A CHRISTMAS WITH CHRIST

A Christmas with Christ
Finding Joy Each December

ALEX BASILE

ST PAULS

Library of Congress Cataloging-in-Publication Data

Basile, Alex.
  A Christmas with Christ : finding joy each December / by Alex Basile.
    p. cm.
  ISBN 978-0-8189-1338-9
  1. Christmas. 2. Simplicity—Religious aspects—Christianity. I. Title.
  BV45.B325 2011
  263'.915—dc23

                              2011017943

Produced and designed in the United States of America by the
Fathers and Brothers of the Society of St. Paul,
2187 Victory Boulevard, Staten Island, New York 10314-6603
as part of their communications apostolate.

ISBN 10: 0-8189-1338-X
ISBN 13: 978-0-8189-1338-9

Printing Information:

Current Printing - first digit   3   4   5   6   7   8   9   10

Year of Current Printing - first year shown

                                          2019

Let Your goodness Lord appear to us,
that we made in Your image, conform ourselves to it.
In our own strength we cannot imitate Your majesty, power,
and wonder nor is it fitting for us to try. But Your mercy reaches
from the heavens through the clouds to the earth below.
You have come to us as a small child,
but You have brought us the greatest of all gifts,
the gift of eternal love. Caress us with Your tiny hands,
embrace us with Your tiny arms and pierce our hearts
with Your soft, sweet cries.

St. Bernard of Clairvaux (1090-1153)

Table of Contents

Acknowledgments

*Many thanks to Justin Michelena and Jeff Harris
for the cover design.*

To my parents, who made every Christmas a magical experience.

*To my good friend and mentor, Father Thomas Cardone, S.M.,
who adds his spiritual touch to every project.*

*To my beautiful wife Allison,
who teaches me the grace of Christ every day.*

*I dedicate this book to my children Alex and Maggie.
Your joy makes every day Christmas.*

Preface

As a young person I could always remember the preparations for Christmas that began with the First Sunday of Advent. The Advent wreath, the Jesse tree and the spiritual Advent calendars were engaging symbols that cultivated a sense of expectation for the birth of Jesus on Christmas. Doing good deeds to welcome Jesus were an important part of Advent for children. Each deed was rewarded with the chance to put a piece of straw in an empty manger so that when Jesus appeared he would have a comfortable bed.

Many years after this as a teacher, I began to sense the loss of the liturgical season of Advent in the lives of Christians; however, I kept in mind that the message of Christmas would be like a never extinguished flame on a candle. How could we lose Christmas?

Sadly enough as a culture, as time has gone by, we have lost the birth of Jesus and the meaning of Christmas to the secularism of the present age. What are we to do?

The answer is found in Alex Basile's *A Christmas with Christ*. Alex has written this book as an aid to restore the true meaning of the birth of Christ to Christians today. What has become a holiday, a season of consumerism and secularism is now countered by Alex as he presents reflections and numerous suggestions to renew the spiritual dimension of Christmas.

Each chapter concludes with thought provoking questions that invite the person to meditation, personal challenge and a call to holiness. Christmas is more than a sentimental moment that touches our hearts; but a call to a spiritual work that overflows from a faith rooted in the person of Jesus.

Father Thomas A. Cardone, S.M.

Introduction

Each December, the world transforms into a kinder, gentler place. For the young and old alike, Christmas is a magical experience. Today, Christians and even non-Christians wrap their hearts around the generosity of Christmas. Everything seems different during the month of December. We rise to a different level at this time of year. As Washington Irving stated,

> Christmas is the season for kindling the fire of hospitality in the hall, the genial flame of charity in the heart.

Even though we grow weary towards the end of another year, the preparation for Christmas seems to rejuvenate us.

Every year, society prepares for the commercial season of Christmas earlier than the year before. The catalogs start to arrive in September. By Halloween, the garland and lights are placed in the local shopping mall. Being children at heart, we never hesitate to jump onto the express lane that puts us into the midst of Christmas even though the calendar may still read "November." We pack our schedules with various activities and by the first week in January we reiterate the same old sentiment, "Christmas came and went by too quickly!" Sucked into the frenzy of the season, we fail to stand back and take it all in.

We do not take time to reflect on the deeply profound beauty of the Incarnation. We overlook God's sacrifice as He leaves the perfection and glory of heaven to dwell amongst a selfish and blind humanity. We forget to include Jesus as we make our preparations for Christmas. The birthday party is in place and we never invite the guest of honor. As the days grow shorter, we leave Christ out in the cold on the darkest nights of the year. We tend to our family Yuletide traditions with tremendous planning and effort. We relegate prayer and reflection to church, the only place that shelters us from the commercial chaos and provides the space to ponder God's intervention in the world. If we integrate Christ into our decorating, our baking, our shopping and everything else we do as we ready our homes for Christmas, our hearts would be properly disposed as well.

The focus on consumerism distracts humanity from the true meaning of the birth of the Savior. Society has fused the celebrations of Halloween, Thanksgiving, Christmas and New Year's into a secular season called "The Holidays." The religious element of Christmas has been replaced by a generic shopping period that coincides nicely with the corporate quarterly reports. I am not speaking here of the blatant war against Christmas where certain factions of society remove sacred symbols in the name of "tolerance." Instead, I refer to the unintentional exclusion of Jesus from our lives as Christmas approaches. The religious dimension of Christmas should not be saved until we enter our parish church. The purpose of *A Christmas with Christ* is to serve as a reminder that including Jesus in our activities during Advent and Christmas can make everything special. Every tradition, party and family gathering will take on new meaning.

Perhaps, our first piece of advice can come from a sign displayed in Nordstrom's explaining why they had not yet decorated for Christmas even though it was a week before Thanksgiving: "We only celebrate one holiday at a time." So celebrate your inner child on Halloween and remember the Feast of All Saints and pray for those who have died on the Feast of All Souls! Understand that gratitude is an essential spiritual attitude as you gather and recall all God's blessings on Thanksgiving. We should live for the moment and make the most out of each special occasion as it emerges.

Liturgically, Christians spend the four weeks prior to Christmas readying themselves for the coming of Jesus at His birth. Because of the elaborate nature of our preparations, society's version of Advent is lost. Doing too many things at one time distracts us from our primary goal. Multitasking has become an art. But no matter how proficient we are at juggling the different aspects of life, some things must suffer. Unfortunately during the flurry of Christmas, we lose sight of the star of the main event.

The chapters of this book recall the various components of our Christmas preparations and celebrations. Our goal should be to return to the simplicity of the stable in Bethlehem. The birth of Jesus went virtually ignored when He entered the world as a poor and humble servant. Today, we show Him only a little more attention than the people of Israel even in the fanfare of our celebrations. English poet, Leigh Hunt reminds us of our practical need to focus:

> Fail not to call to mind in the course of the 25th of this month, that the Divinest Heart that ever walked the earth was born on that day; then smile and enjoy yourselves for the rest of it; for mirth is also of heaven's making.

Christmas arouses the weary and lightens the worried. God must get great pleasure from our rejoicing in the birth of His Son. As we saw in His ministry, no one loved a party more than Jesus, so I doubt He would discourage us from pulling out all the stops as we remember His birthday. Create a celebration fit for a king, but keep the King of Kings in mind as you put the final touches on your home. Make Christmas memories each year as you gather your friends and family together. Set a place for Jesus at your table.

At the end of every chapter of this book, there are questions and journal space for quiet moments of reflection. Take the opportunity during Advent and Christmas to ponder some topics that may assist you in making this a more fulfilling time of year. I hope that A Christmas with Christ helps you in your celebration of Christmas for years to come. Spend some time to answer the questions. Pick up the book again after Christmas and see whether or not you were able to accomplish some of your goals. Give a copy to a family member or a friend to help them finding deeper meaning this Christmas.

May the birth of Jesus open your heart and mind to the wonder of God. May you discover the road to Bethlehem and the true path to His stable.

For a Quiet Moment

What do I need to change in this year's celebration of Christmas so it has a greater Christ dimension?

Christmas is all about people. Who are the people in my life that need more attention?

_____

_____

_____

_____

_____

_____

_____

_____

_____

A CHRISTMAS WITH CHRIST

1

What Goes Around, Comes Around

> Advent, like its cousin Lent, is a season for prayer and reformation of our hearts. Since it comes at wintertime, fire is a fitting sign to help us celebrate Advent. If Christ is to come more fully into our lives this Christmas, if God is to become really incarnate for us, then fire will have to be present in our prayer. Our worship and devotion will have to stoke the kind of fire in our souls that can truly change our hearts. Ours is a great responsibility not to waste this Advent time.
>
> Edward Hays, *A Pilgrim's Almanac*

When people look to writers of the Christian world, one of the most profound, yet overlooked, voices is the one of Gilbert Keith Chesterton. G.K. Chesterton offered some of the most practical advice for us. Chesterton lived "large" both literally and figuratively. With a frame of well over six feet tall and weighing more than 300 pounds, he lived to enjoy the finer things in life. He would often frequent his favorite pub to sample some of the many beers, wines and spirits there as well as to delight in a fulfilling meal. Chesterton recognized the value of using the material items of this world to become closer to God and others. He also knew that when we do not place the proper value on these things, it could be deadly. In an article he wrote for *The Illustrated London News* called "The Rituals of Christmas" on Christmas Eve in 1927, we find:

> All ceremony depends on symbol; and all symbols have been vulgarized and made stale by the commercial conditions of our time.... Of all these faded and falsified symbols, the most melancholy example is the ancient symbol of the flame. In every civilized age and country, it has been a natural thing to talk of some great festival on which "the town was illuminated." There is no meaning nowadays in saying that the town was illuminated.... The whole town is illuminated already, but not for noble things. It is illuminated solely to insist on the immense importance of trivial and material things, blazoned from motives entirely mercenary.... It has not destroyed the difference between light and darkness, but it has allowed the lesser light to put out the greater.... Our streets are in permanent dazzle, and our minds in a permanent darkness.

Even in the early 20th century, Chesterton saw how people around him distorted Christmas. Towns went to great lengths to illuminate their streets and homes, yet they remained in darkness; people filled their plates, but their hunger lingered; they grew in wealth only to dwell in the poverty of the soul. Chesterton understood the persistent problem of the ages: humanity's lethal attraction to harmful materialism. Today, we can't seem to take our eyes off the television as it promotes the glitz and glamour of Hollywood. Society entices us with the newest cars, sleekest technology and trendiest clothing. Materialism and hedonism lure us away from worshiping our God as we ought. They drag us into an arena where we will only find misery. Chesterton knew that many

Christians had forgotten the true meaning of Christmas. "People are losing the power to enjoy Christmas through identifying it with enjoyment," he stated in his essay "The New War on Christmas." We assume that society's struggle with Christmas is a new one. However, even as Chesterton made these remarks in 1925, he was dealing with an old issue. If Chesterton lived today, he would have realized that in the midst of our baking, decorating, wrapping and partying, our need for an anchor during the turbulence of December still exists. That anchor is Christ. Without the intervention of Christ in our world, we remain desolate and hopeless. Advent is our chance to look forward to great possibilities. The theologian and spiritual writer Dietrich Bonhoeffer said this about Advent:

> A prison cell, in which one waits, hopes... and is completely dependent on the fact that the door of freedom has to be opened from the outside, it's not a bad picture of Advent.

For Christians, Christmas would be incomplete without the preparatory Season of Advent. In Latin, *ad venio* means "coming." Each year, we spend the weeks before Christmas preparing the way for the Lord. As life becomes cluttered with the materialistic demands of society, Advent provides us with balance. God wants us to remember His Son, as our greatest gift. In 1986, Cardinal Joseph Ratzinger (Pope Benedict XVI) spoke about Advent's message of goodness:

> Advent is concerned with that very connection between memory and hope which is so necessary to man. Advent's intention is to awaken the most profound and basic emotional memory within us, namely, the memory of the God who became a child. This is a healing memory; it brings hope. The purpose of the Church's year is

> continually to rehearse her great history of memories, to awaken the heart's memory so that it can discern the star of hope. (*Seek That Which Is Above*, 1986)

The Church calls us to cleanse our soul in order to make it a suitable home for the Redeemer of the world. Advent starts the Church year and for Christians it is a time of new beginnings. The emergence of Christ in our world changed everything. Sin and death have no power over humanity. The selflessness of God broke the momentum of our downward spiral away from Him. His presence in our world gives us great hope, a chance for everlasting happiness. The *Catechism of the Catholic Church* explains the importance of the season:

> When the Church celebrates the liturgy of Advent each year, she makes present the ancient expectancy of the Messiah, for by sharing in the long preparation for the Savior's first coming, the faithful renew their ardent desire for his second coming. (CCC 524)

The Advent Roundup

Advent begins on the Sunday closest to the last day of November, the feast of St. Andrew the Apostle (November 30). The season lasts four weeks. During Mass, the celebrant wears purple vestments. While the Gloria is omitted from the Mass, the Alleluia is still spoken or sung. On Gaudete Sunday, you may see rose-colored vestments being worn and flowers placed on the altar.

The roots of Advent can be traced to Spain where a synod modeled the preparatory season for Christmas after Lent. Advent consisted of fasting, prayer and mandatory church attendance. Instead of Christmas, this version of Advent anticipated the feast of the Epiphany. In 6th century France, the Council of Macon stated that Christians should fast on Monday, Wednesday and Friday.

Tradition tells us that Pope St. Gelasius formalized the Season of Advent, which lasted five Sundays. Later St. Gregory I composed prayers, antiphons, readings and responses that centralized the theme of this season. St. Gregory VII reduced the number of Sundays in Advent to the four that we are accustomed to today.

When we enter a church, we find the Advent wreath as our primary symbol. The four candles inserted into the wreath represent Jesus as the light of the world. Three of the candles are violet (the traditional color of Advent) and one is rose-colored for Gaudete Sunday, the third Sunday of Advent. Rose symbolizes our anticipation of Christ's first coming into the world as well as His second coming and judgment at the end of time. The circular shape reminds worshipers that God's love has neither beginning nor end. His salvation remains constant throughout the history of humanity. The evergreen wreath symbolizes the everlasting life provided by our faith in God. The pinecones, nuts and fruit that adorn the wreath commemorate the Resurrection of Jesus. These adornments literally spread the seeds of new life, a life that Christians celebrate in Jesus Christ.

Advent changes the way we see the world. It tells us that God truly desires to be part of us. In order for us to join His kingdom, we may have to change radically just as He changed radically to enter our world. We must prepare for His arrival. As we would ready ourselves for any visitor to our homes, Advent is a time to clean up ourselves spiritually. Various situations often change the way we see Advent. This occurred to Father Alfred Delp, a Jesuit priest who was killed by the Nazis for opposing Hitler. As he sat in prison he pondered the power of this season:

> The Advent message comes out of an encounter of man with the absolute, the final, the gospel. It is for us the message that shakes so that in the end of the world we shall be shaken. ...if we are inwardly incapable of being

genuinely shaken, if we become obstinate and hard and superficial and cheap, then God will himself intervene in world events and teach us what it means to be placed in this agitation and be stirred inwardly.... Advent is a time when we ought to be shaken and brought to a realization of ourselves. The necessary condition for the fulfillment of Advent is the renunciation of the presumptuous attitudes and alluring dreams in which and by means of which we always build ourselves imaginary worlds. In this way we force reality to take us to itself by force – by force in much pain and suffering.

Alfred Delp wanted to make us conscious of our need for dependence on God. He knew that this is impossible to do on our own. Because of our attraction to the superficial, the Father sent us His Son to show us the truth. God's intervention shakes us back to reality. Use this solemn season to emphasize the importance of Christ in your life. When the parties, shopping, baking, card writing and other preparations start to become a distraction, remind yourself and others that the love of God is the main reason for the celebration. As Advent comes around each year, make a new beginning.

For a Quiet Moment

What is your earliest memory of Jesus during Advent or Christmas? Write an Advent prayer including your spiritual goals for the next four weeks.

_____

_____

_____

_____

2

The Christmas Spirit

I will honor Christmas in my heart, and try to keep it
all the year. I will live in the Past, the Present, and the
Future. The Spirits of all Three shall strive within me.
I will not shut out the lessons that they teach. Oh, tell
me I may sponge away the writing on this stone!
Ebenezer Scrooge in A Christmas Carol

Ebenezer Scrooge lived a miserable existence. He built the prison
of his solitude one brick at a time. Ebenezer wasn't always a selfish
and nasty individual. He evolved into a person who cared about
no one but himself. At one time, he had many friends and even
met the true love of his life. But Ebenezer soon found something
he loved more than anyone else: money. He worked endless hours
to accumulate as much of it as he could. It became the center of
his life, his god. He would forsake everyone and everything in his
pursuit of money. When we meet Ebenezer, the glory days of his
business are long gone. His partner, Jacob Marley, had died several
years before. Scrooge and his assistant Bob Cratchit worked in a
cold, damp and dimly lit office. Scrooge refused to spend the money
he needed to sufficiently light and heat the place.

Money has a different effect on different people. Some become extremely generous with their accumulation of wealth, while some hold on to their money for dear life. Ebenezer's worship of money drove him to overlook the poverty of others, and worse yet, his own spiritual poverty. Scrooge truly hated Christmas. He had become the antithesis of "peace and good will to men."

> "If I could work my will," said Scrooge indignantly, "every idiot who goes about with 'Merry Christmas' on his lips, should be boiled with his own pudding, and buried with a stake of holly through his heart. He should!"

Christmas is the feast of generosity and love. The spirit of the season makes us contemplate life. We may never have the pleasure of the spiritual visitors that came to visit Scrooge on that Christmas Eve; however, every sight and sound in the days that lead up to Christmas should remind us of God's infinite love brought to life in Bethlehem. As the world appears different at Christmas, so do our hearts as they grow in the outward flowing of God's saving grace that He bestows upon the world. The feeling of Christmas should not end as the year ends and we move into January. The joy of Christmas can become a permanent part of the way that we live. Our feelings must evolve into an active faith in order for us to live the message of Christmas. As Advent starts the liturgical year, it should mark a beginning to a conversion in our lives. We can use it as a time to make real changes. How can we change as we move beyond Christmas into the New Year?

Adopt the simplicity of the stable. Jesus entered this world with absolutely nothing; we, however, rely on a world of abundance and plenitude. Pare down the purposeless things in your life and recognize essential needs. The Christmas story illustrates the importance of finding joy in absolute humility. The Son of God did not hesitate to have common farm animals present at His birth. He chose to arrive unnoticed, even though His life would touch everyone. Follow the lifestyle of the Holy Family from Bethlehem to Nazareth and enjoy simplicity in your own personal faith journey.

Focus on the importance of others. The most beautiful quality of Christmas is that it makes a human race that has a tendency to constantly look inward, concentrate on others. We worry about buying the perfect gift for someone we care about. We stress over a meal that we prepare for family. Shift the emphasis to others in your life. Make your relationships a priority. Gather around the table to celebrate each moment that you have together. Once the warm fires of Christmas expire, work to rekindle the spark of a lost romance with a spouse or to renew a friendship with an old acquaintance. Continue the conversations when the party ends and the decorations have been stored back in the attic. Offer your companionship to those who only seem to receive an invitation but once a year. Do as Jesus did, as He pulled people from the fringe back into the circle of friendship.

Approach life with childlike wonder. We become jaded and skeptical because we've been disappointed so many times. When you look into a child's eyes at Christmas, you witness a faith and trust that we must rediscover as we grow older. Restore trust in your relationships with God and others. Hand yourself over to Christ and surrender your life to Him. Remember the enthusiasm of your childhood. Stop worrying about what others think about you. Take on a new perspective and live life as if you are experiencing it for the first time.

Celebrate Christ every day. The birth of Jesus reminds us that He is the centerpiece of humanity and that our world must revolve around Him. Worship and adore Him throughout the year. Make your presence at Mass your gift to Him. Spread His joy to others and sow the seeds of God's love along your journey. Show the world that the peace and joy of Christmas can be experienced at all times. Become a messenger of the Good News. Reintroduce

Jesus to a culture that seems to have forgotten about Him. If Jesus is the vine, we as the branches can't live apart from Him. Unite yourself and others to Jesus and experience a spiritual magic that will not end.

When in doubt, love! People appear to be more open to practice acts of charity for the sake of others at Christmas. Practice love in all of your relationships every day. When confused on how to act or what to do, make others a priority. The goodwill that permeates humanity may vanish as the bills arrive in the weeks after Christmas, but we cannot let this diminish the beauty of His birth. Love must grow daily in order for us to be successful in our relationships. Allow the love of Christmas to change the way you relate to others.

Christmas can soften the hardest of hearts. Ebenezer Scrooge awoke from his sleep on Christmas morning as a changed man. We have the possibility to emerge from Christmas as people who are more aware of those in need. Our challenge is to remain diligent in our efforts to assist them. Scrooge came to the realization that his isolation had killed him spiritually. God created us to be in communion with one another. If we are to love others as Christ loved, we must open the door to our hearts. Love can't pour forth at Christmas and stop flowing when it ends. The fountain of love should gush from deep within us at all times. Just as we are amazed by Ebenezer Scrooge's transformation, we will be astounded by the change in us.

Examine your life and see where you stand. Do you find yourself emulating Jesus or Scrooge? We may be closer to Scrooge than we think. Evaluate how you use your money. Is it used with goodness or has it become your god? Do you ease the burdens of those around you or do you cause them? Many of us suffer from the same spiritual blindness that afflicted Scrooge. We become numb to the envy, laziness, greed and apathy that capture our souls. Selfishness consumes us until we no longer feel its effects.

We believe we are making great strides only to realize that we have deteriorated as human beings. Allow the God of love to awaken you to a new day and a new way of living. Cultivate a relationship that begins with an encounter at the stable and culminates in glory with Him at the Resurrection. Find the inner peace of Christmas that fills your entire life with joy. Grow with Jesus as He grows from child to man. Look to Him and ask for the courage to become a true disciple. Be a voice of hope in times of despair. Bring the warmth of Christmas into the cold and uncaring world. Make your transformation this Christmas.

For A Quiet Moment

Am I a comfortable Christian or a challenged one?

The stable and the Gospel call us to grow and stretch beyond our self-imposed limitations. What selfish characteristics do I need to change?

Do I find strength in being with others or do I retreat in isolation?

_____

_____

_____

_____

_____

_____

_____

_____

_____

_____

_____

_____

_____

3

Behold the Wood

That chosen and royal race must live up to the dignity
of its regeneration, must love what the Father loves, and
in naught disagree with its Maker, lest the Lord should
again say: "I have begotten and raised up sons, but they
have scorned Me: the ox knoweth his owner and the ass
his master's crib; but Israel hath not known Me and My
people hath not acknowledged Me."   *Pope St. Leo I*

In 1987, I traveled to Germany on vacation. One day, we decided
to do some shopping to pass the time. I passed a small wood
carver's shop in the tiny Bavarian town we visited. A small hand
carved Nativity set grabbed my attention in the window. The
artist had created a stable that resembled a rustic alpine chalet.
The uniqueness of the stable and figures prompted my desire for
an instant purchase. Growing up, my parents always gave me the
privilege of setting up our family's Nativity set. It was a thrill to
find a piece of art that would become an instant heirloom and part
of our family Christmas tradition forever. So with my credit card
in hand, I entered the store. I pointed out the Nativity set to the
young woman behind the counter. As she went into the stock room
to bring out my newfound treasure, I beamed with pride. When

the clerk returned, she noticed the credit card in my hand. "I'm sorry," she said apologetically, "but we accept only cash." "Oh," I said sadly. With not enough cash to make my purchase, I left the store dejected. I vowed that one day I would return and make my purchase. The following year I fulfilled my promise and although the shop did not have the exact Nativity set that I had seen the previous year, I found another magnificent crèche that has become the centerpiece of our Christmas decorations.

The infancy narratives of Matthew and Luke inspire us at Christmas. Their telling of the birth of Jesus also moved St. Francis. In a visit to the small town of Grecio in 1223, Francis desired to inspire the inhabitants with a novel, yet solemn approach to celebrating the Nativity of the Lord. Fearing criticism and the perception that he was making light of such a sacred event, Francis even sought the permission of the Pope. St. Francis enlisted the assistance of his friend Giovanni Vellita, a Grecio landowner, to help him pick the perfect spot for the Christmas event. They placed a manger between an ox and a donkey. As tradition tells us, Francis used the manger as the altar. The members of the congregation listened as he sang the Gospel account and preached to the crowd about the Nativity of Christ the King. Francis referred to Jesus as "the little babe of Bethlehem." As Giovanni watched Francis, he experienced a vision where he saw a baby in a manger laying lifelessly until awakened by Francis. St. Bonaventure who wrote an account of the life of Francis attested to the veracity of the story:

> ...Nor was this vision untrue, for by the grace of God through his servant Blessed Francis, Christ was awakened in many hearts where formerly He slept.

News of Francis' wonderful devotion to the Nativity spread. It gave Christians a tangible image of the birth of the Savior. By the Middle Ages, churches in Spain, France, Italy and Germany included nativity plays in their Christmas celebrations. In the 18th century, carved representations were being sold throughout Europe. The Italian city of Naples became known for creating the most beautiful hand carved Nativity sets during this time. After World War I, churches, towns and businesses started to display life-size nativity scenes. Today, we continue this tradition in our homes.

As we set up a crèche in our homes, we need to take time to reflect on the miracle of Christmas. Each component of the stable represents an important message in Salvation History.

The Shepherds

The angels proclaimed the good news of the birth of Jesus to the lowly shepherds. Living out in the fields away from society, they were considered outcasts. St. Luke included them in his gospel to illustrate that Jesus came to everyone: Jew or gentile; rich or poor; popular or unpopular. Jesus spent His entire earthly life reaching out to the unwanted and unloved. They became part of His inner circle. As you gaze upon the manger in your home, notice the proximity of the outcasts to the King of Kings and reflect on how you can better include the forgotten into your world.

The Angels

Heavenly messengers brought the incredible news of God's glory to the earth. The Angels remind us to spread the message of God's peace and love. We are also enlisted by God to bring heaven to earth. How many times do we hesitate to show others that we follow Christ? Make no excuses for being a disciple of Jesus. Bring Christ to others through your words and deeds. Be a herald of the Christian message.

The Magi

Known also as the three Kings, the Magi seemed to be the most mysterious visitors to the Christ Child. We assume that there were three wise men because of the three gifts presented to Jesus. Curiously, St. Augustine and St. John Chrysostom taught that there were twelve kings. Tradition tells us their names and the gifts that they presented to the Holy Family. Melchior, the King of Arabia, brought a vessel of gold. He is usually represented as the oldest. Gaspar, the King of Tarsus, gave the present of myrrh, a burial spice. He is seen as the youngest of the Magi and usually depicted as beardless. Balthazar, the African King of Ethiopia, bestowed frankincense upon Jesus. Each gift is symbolic: gold reminds us of the kingship of Jesus; frankincense the prayers of the high priest; myrrh foreshadows the death of Jesus. The Magi came a great distance to pay homage to the Messiah. Their journey and presence at the stable shows us the importance of our need to go to Jesus. Our desire to have Him in our lives sometimes requires us to make tremendous sacrifices. How far will we go to make Him part of our lives? Do whatever you can to follow His light.

The Animals Around Jesus

To those who heard the story of Christmas for the first time, their reaction must have been, "Surely, the Son of God deserved better than this!" When we observe the animals and the pristine hay of our Nativity sets, we often forget about the realities of the stable. The stench from animal waste slips our mind. Our tidy and clean manger at home only partially represents the real humility of Christ's birth. Homeless and alone, Mary and Joseph had no choice but to give birth amidst the squalor of the animals. The Lord chose the simplest of creatures to surround His Son when He joined us. The God of All chose to forego any of the luxuries of this life from the moment of His birth until His death. God need not sit on His heavenly throne in order for us to proclaim His greatness. Our culture believes the bigger, brighter, the better when it comes to celebrating Christmas. We can learn how to find fulfillment by studying the birth of Jesus. Practice the humility of Christ and find true joy. Peel away the superficial layers to discover His simplicity and peace.

The role of Jesus as a servant is evident from the moment of His birth. The 16th century poet, John Donne, spoke about how the sacrifice of Jesus began at His birth:

> The whole life of Christ was a continual passion; others die martyrs but Christ was born a martyr. He found a Golgotha, where He was crucified, even in Bethlehem, where He was born; for to His tenderness then the straws were almost as sharp as the thorns after, and the manger as uneasy at first as the cross at last. His birth and His death were but one continual act, and His Christmas Day and His Good Friday are but the evening and the morning of the same day.

The stable became the starting point of the journey to Calvary. Jesus gives Himself to us completely from His very first moment on earth. As the prophet Simeon reminded us as Jesus was presented in the Temple, we should anticipate His death at even the very beginning of His life.

This Christmas, as we place our Nativity sets upon the mantel, the table or under the tree, meditate on how the glory of God transformed into earthly beauty. Make sure to put the manger scene in the location where everyone can easily see it. My former pastor kept his Nativity set on his mantel all year long. When parishioners questioned him about why he had not yet stored it away with the rest of his decorations, he answered, "We should celebrate the gift of God's love every day."

St. Augustine explained that the presence of Jesus in the manger requires incredible contemplation:

> He lies in a manger but He holds the world. He nurses at His mother's breasts, but He feeds the angels. He is wrapped in swaddling clothes, but He gives the garments of immortality. He is given milk but at the same time adored. He finds no room at the inn, but He builds a temple for Himself in the hearts of those who believe.

Study the stable and see how He was humbled to exalt us. He became weak to provide us with strength. He has died so that we may live forever. Keep the manger in your heart and on your mind all year long. Permit the wood of the manger to lead you to the wood of the cross. Remember that the sacrifice of Christ is not a one-day event. It begins in Bethlehem and culminates in Jerusalem. Let it grow in your heart daily.

For a Quiet Moment

Take time to look and meditate on your stable or crèche. Are you an Angel, a Shepherd or one of the Magi?

The Shepherds bring their sheep, and the Magi their gifts of gold, frankincense and myrrh. What personal gifts and talents do you place before Christ?

How can the manger become like the Cross in helping me become closer to Christ?

_____

_____

_____

_____

_____

4

Blue Christmas

Isn't it funny that at Christmas something in you gets
so lonely for – I don't know what exactly – but it's something that you don't mind so much not having at other
times.   *Kate L. Bosher*

In my senior year of high school, I was offered a job at the local
delicatessen. Retail business requires its workers to invest a copious
amount of hours. One of the owners, Bernie, adamantly held to
the store's tradition of remaining open on every holiday, including Christmas. As a clerk, I avoided working on holidays like the
plague. Holidays were important to me, and I wanted to relax and
enjoy these days. When I purchased the store, Bernie implored me
to hold faithful to this tradition. Honoring his request, I became
the keeper of the holidays. Thanksgiving and Christmas were very
busy at the deli as shoppers came in for last-minute necessities.

People appreciated my willingness to open since the major
stores remain closed during this time. As time passed, I realized
that these were great days to work. People who came into the store
shared in the spirit of the day. They would wish you a "Happy
Thanksgiving" or "Merry Christmas" and expressed their gratitude
for our service throughout the year. However, not every shopper
experienced a lighter mood on these days. Some felt more alone

than ever during this time of year. There would always be a customer who would place their order for a meager quarter pound of turkey that would serve as the centerpiece for their feast. A time of community was overshadowed by their isolation. Other people seemed miserable even though they spent this time surrounded by friends and family. These people didn't need to spend their holidays alone to utter, "Bah humbug!" These Grinches failed to rise to the joy of the holiday. Some people suffer from clinical depression that must be treated by a professional. Here, I am referring to the person who gets derailed by Christmas.

Christmas can transport some people to an uncomfortable place. The rush of emotions that accompanies this season can paralyze some people. The endless gatherings may serve as a reminder of our failed relationships. Our clogged schedules can accentuate our inability to accomplish vital tasks on our plate. Christmas makes us evaluate our lives. Looking inward may cause existential frustration. Like George Bailey in *It's A Wonderful Life*, we question our self-worth. We examine where we have been and wonder where life's path will lead. I personally have experienced sudden despair during the great season of joy. Worrying about finances or the pressures of my job has robbed me of celebrating as I should. The Christmas blues can affect anyone. We assume that feelings of elation must accompany the decorations and fanfare. A person can experience isolation even though loved ones surround them. There is an expectation that we must rise to the occasion. How can we remedy the Christmas blues? There are some simple solutions to fighting the anxiety that Christmas may present.

Eliminate the nonessentials

Our culture tends to promote overindulgence. Pare down the frills when you plan a party or special dinner. People appreciate the fact that you have invited them into your home and that you have made the effort to prepare a meal for them. Focus instead on your family and your guests. Instead of being glued to the stove and stuck in the kitchen, plan ahead so that you can spend quality time with your company.

You can minimize the craziness in your schedule by picking and choosing the events that you want to and need to attend. We sometimes feel as if we cannot refuse an invitation. This results in jumping on the treadmill that exhausts us during Christmas. Prioritize the invitations as they pour in during the late days of November and in early December. People respect an honest and sincere response, even if it's a "no" to an invitation. If my wife and I are not able to attend a party this year, we try to make that a priority the next.

Stay in the mix

Plan events with important people in your life. Our greatest fulfillment is found in our relationships. Spending time with the people we love and who love us, can provide us with an instant boost. Stop avoiding situations that push you out of your comfort zone. Entering a room where you do not know many people can be scary. Throw yourself into social situations. Expand your circle of friends and acquaintances by being willing to venture into the unknown.

Focus on the true meaning of the season

When we feel overwhelmed, we should remember Mary and Joseph as they entered the chaos of Bethlehem. We can find solace in the most difficult moments when we focus on Christ and let ourselves fall into His arms. When this season seems to be spinning out of control, seek His peace and consolation. Stepping into the stable requires us to shift the focus from ourselves and onto others. Just as God abandoned His glory for the meekness of the manger, we can overcome all things through His love.

Be gentle with yourself

Many times we create expectations that we can never live up to. We become our toughest critics. When the decorations are not the way we pictured them or our dinner doesn't look the way it did when Martha Stewart prepared it, put a positive spin on your situation. It is not worth beating yourself up. Look instead at the blessing of being given the opportunity to come together with your loved ones. Ease the worries of the season by ceasing to put undue pressure on yourself. Do everything with great love and every aspect of your celebration will be perfect.

Create a joyful atmosphere

The amount of decorations, the number of courses in a meal or the amount of people at our party does not determine our happiness at Christmas. The true jubilation of Christmas supersedes all of the material components of the feast. The warmth of good conversation and the laughter resonating throughout your home quickly elevates the mood of the celebration. Put on the stereo and create a soundtrack that makes the world sing along. Cultivate a joy that is contagious. Send people from your home filled with the hope of Christ.

Sometimes when we do not feel particularly joyful, we need to find a reason to smile. We may need to dig deep down within ourselves to discover our blessings. Adopt the joy of Mary and Joseph and share the wonder of charity that begins with God. As children, we counted the days until the arrival of Christmas. As adults there may be times when we can't wait until it's over. When the Christmas blues make us resemble the Grinch rather than St. Nick, we should take time to regroup and rediscover the wonder we experienced as kids. When the moments of desperation drive us to wish away Christmas instead of embracing it, we should look beyond the things that overwhelm us. Dr. Seuss understood how the season affects some people. But he also saw hope through the true meaning of Christmas:

> And the Grinch, with his Grinch-feet ice cold in the snow, stood puzzling and puzzling, how could it be so? It came without ribbons. It came without tags. It came without packages, boxes or bags. And he puzzled and puzzled 'till his puzzler was sore. Then the Grinch thought of something he hadn't thought of before. "What if Christmas," he thought, "doesn't come from a store? What if Christmas, perhaps, means a little bit more?"

The child in the manger serves as a reminder that we can find happiness in the simplest aspects of life. Don't let your preparations for Christmas overwhelm you. Let His joy bring you joy. Surround yourself with His love in the love of others.

For A Quiet Moment

Do you have any symptoms of Blue Christmas?

Do you have to be everything to everyone at Christmas?

Do you look for a false sense of Christmas happiness rather than a true sense of inner joy that comes from Christ alone?

_____

_____

_____

_____

_____

_____

_____

5

Shop 'til You Drop

Wretched excess is an unfortunate human trait that
turns a perfectly good idea such as Christmas into a
frenzy of last-minute shopping.   *Jon Anderson*

Children can offer a unique perspective on a situation. They have
the ability to see the world as it really is. Last year my eight-year-old
son, Alex, provided us with a Christmas Epiphany. As we packed
the car in preparation for our Christmas visit to my parents' house,
Alex could not comprehend that there could possibly be more
presents to unwrap. "More gifts?" he wondered, "I already have so
many things!" Every year we stack our treasures generously under
our trees. Access to extended credit permits us to spend beyond
our means. We no longer purchase gifts proportionate to a family
budget; instead, we shop hoping to outdo our last exchange. The
infinite ads and circulars heighten our impulse to overindulge.

The tradition of giving gifts at Christmas can be traced to the
Magi. People have decided to copy their majestic gesture to the
newborn King. In the days of the Roman Empire, people exchanged
gifts during the feast of the winter solstice and at the New Year.
Romans believed that good fortune would come their way in the
coming year if they exhibited generosity to each other. This tradi-

tion continued as Romans converted and joined the Christian faith. As the Roman Empire evaporated, so did the practice of giving gifts at Christmas. People did, however, continue their tradition of giving presents on New Year's Day, which lasted until the reign of Queen Victoria.

During the Middle Ages some central and eastern Europeans honored the feast of St. Nicholas (December 6) by giving gifts to children. Later, monarchs created a law in which the poorest subjects had to pay tribute to their king and rich lords on Christmas Day. In the 11th and 12th centuries, good King Wenceslaus and William the Conqueror reversed this tradition by distributing goods to the less fortunate and donating a sum of money to the poor. In the 16th century, Germans followed the tradition of St. Nicholas and Wenceslaus by anonymously giving gifts to one other.

Puritan ideals prevented the exchange of gifts from taking root in England and the American colonies. They felt that presents should be given only to the baby Jesus. Religious leaders frowned upon a formal celebration of Christmas. Christians were told to reflect on the solemn feast with reverence, not exultation. The closest that people came to giving gifts at Christmas was emulating the wise men on the feast of the Epiphany. When Clement Clarke Moore's *The Night Before Christmas* popularized the notion of Santa Claus, gift giving finally became widespread in America and England. Today millions of people make the pilgrimage to the mall spending billions of dollars daily during the shopping season leading up to Christmas. Shopping need not be a purely secular ritual paying homage to the gods of commercialism. Here are some ideas to make the shopping process faith filled:

Create a communal event out of your shopping experience

As much as I enjoy roaming the stores alone, the pressure of finding the perfect gift can be overwhelming and frustrating. Ask a family member or friend to join you as you venture out shopping.

The wait on cashier lines will seem shorter with a companion to pass the time. Finding that hidden treasure will become an adventure instead of drudgery. Use your excursion to the mall to create deeper bonds with loved ones.

Think out of the box

The greatest gift is sacrificing for others. Spend time with a lonely neighbor or relative. The smallest gesture can transform the isolated into people who feel part of the community. Your attentive ear to the lonesome is priceless. A quick chat over a cup of coffee or tea will brighten someone's day. This Christmas, bring the generosity of Jesus to the forgotten and others in need.

Agree to put limits on the gifts that you buy for each other

Buying gifts can easily get out of hand when you start worrying if your gift will adequately match the one that you will receive. Stick to the philosophy of "it's the thought that counts." Focus on real needs, rather than extravagant desires. Once the dust settles, many gifts are filed away in the bin of forgotten items. Keep the simplicity of the first Christmas in mind when you prepare your shopping list.

Choose a shopping venue that suits your style

If crowded stores make you uncomfortable, avoid the frenzy of Black Friday and weekend shopping. Local shops may not offer the same bargains as the chain stores, but you can avoid the crowds that flock to the mall and be pampered by personal service. The Internet allows you to comfortably browse at all hours of day and night. Shopping online offers convenience and selection and may give you more time to spend with your family and friends.

Turn your shopping experience into an act of love. Do not let the commercialism of Christmas make you lose your focus during this special time. Gift giving should enhance your Christmas, not morph it into a nightmare. Construct a reasonable list as you set about your quest for the perfect gifts. When we fall prey to over-blown expectations, we create a Christmas that will never live up to our unrealistic hopes. Capture the love and generosity of God as He gives the world His only Son. Share His benevolence and care in the gifts that you give.

Materialism attempts to distract us from the real reason we enter the mall: to join in the kinship of the selfless Christ. As we jot down ideas on our shopping list, let us contemplate how we can make ourselves truly present to others. Give the gift of yourself to the ones you love. Clear your calendar and take some time to catch up with the people who matter the most. Recognize that life's most precious gifts are friendship, family and faith. When these are wrapped in love, they become our greatest treasures.

For a Quiet Moment

How can I simplify gift giving among my family and friends?

What do I give to the person who has everything?

Did you ever think of making a donation to a particular charity or school in someone's name?

_____

_____

_____

_____

_____

_____

_____

_____

6

Glued to the Tube

Television has proved that people will look at anything rather than each other.
                                              Ann Landers

There are so many times when we exclaim, "There are hundreds of channels and yet there is nothing to watch on TV!" We mindlessly surf the channels to find something to entertain us. As Christmas approaches, we try to discern which programs are worth our precious time. Furthermore, we want to choose shows that enhance our preparation for this sacred time of year. I offer some recommendations that have become part of our family tradition. Each of these movies became classics because of their timeless message to be delivered to people of all faiths.

The Bishop's Wife. Starring David Niven, Loretta Young, and Cary Grant. When a bishop is given the job of building a new cathedral, he forgets about the things that matter most to him. God sends an angel, Dudley, to help Henry remember that his vocation is about his family and his ministry. These two elements provide him with real joy. As Dudley entertains Julia, Henry notices that his wife has transformed back into the "Julia" of old. Julia begs Henry to join her and Dudley on their adventures. Consumed with work, he has no time to do so. Jealousy causes

Henry to confront Dudley and Henry must make some important decisions. The movie reminds us that in the midst of the madness of our lives, our relationship with God and others stands as the true foundation in life.

It's A Wonderful Life. Starring James Stewart and Donna Reed. Good hearted George Bailey constantly has placed others ahead of himself. His generosity cost him the dream of a lucrative career and a hopeful departure from tiny Bedford Falls. George manages his family's financial business and is faced with imprisonment when his uncle loses a deposit before a yearly audit by the bank examiner. George contemplates suicide when he feels that his life has been worthless and it would have been better if he never had existed. God's messenger, Clarence, shows George that the world would have suffered without his presence in it.

We seldom see the effects of our simple acts of kindness. Our smallest gestures of love can change the world. George Bailey makes us conscious of the importance of selflessness. The richness of life accumulates through our relationships with others.

The Nativity. This recent telling of the Christmas story depicts the human struggle in the birth of our Savior. We often forget to ponder the emotions behind this beautiful story. *The Nativity* unveils the humility of peaceful Nazareth and the turbulence of Jerusalem during this period. The journey to Bethlehem is shown not only through the eyes of Mary and Joseph, but through the Magi as well. The movie provides the viewer with a beautiful meditation for the Advent and Christmas seasons. It is a must for every family.

Other movies that depict the birth of Jesus are *The Greatest Story Ever Told* and *Jesus of Nazareth*. Although these movies encompass the entire life of Christ, they give us a realistic glimpse of the beauty surrounding His birth.

Miracle on 34th Street. Starring Edmund Gwenn and Maureen O'Hara. For the skeptic, the question of Santa Claus may be a simple one. But what happens when it seems that the evidence proves otherwise? What do you do when someone claims to be "the man" himself? When Kris Kringle takes the job as the Macy's Santa, many people are called to question their original belief. *Miracle on 34th Street* makes believers out of people young and old.

The Little Drummer Boy (animated). Young Aaron is orphaned when bandits rob his home and murder his parents. Because of what has happened, his hatred has grown for all people. In order to survive, he plays his drum for a traveling show. Through his encounter with the baby Jesus, his heart softens and he understands that he must love others in order to be happy. Many of us allow hatred and disagreements to burden us. Bring yourself to the Christ child and feel your heart become lighter.

The Bells of St. Mary's. Starring Bing Crosby and Ingrid Bergman. This movie was a sequel to the equally popular classic *Going My Way*. It recounts the parish life of Father Charles O'Malley who has become the pastor of St. Mary's. His approach to administering the parish and school finds him at odds with Mother Superior, the school principal. The story brings us back to a time when religious vocations were abundant in the Church. We see the dedication and love which men and women share in their lives serving God. In an age where our society starves for religious life, a movie that initiates the thought of vocations is essential.

A Charlie Brown Christmas (animated). The cartoon appears yearly on network television and remains a favorite Christmas classic. When Charles Schultz created it in the 1960s, commercialism had just begun its competition with the true meaning of Christmas. Today the message behind the show rings truer than ever. This is the perfect show to watch with children as we prepare for Christmas, especially with Linus' recitation of scripture fresh in our minds.

As the reruns of your favorite shows make their appearance in early December, look for the shows to ignite a little spirit in your homes and in the hearts of your loved ones. This season passes by so quickly. Make sure to provide some spiritual nourishment for yourself and others. We do not always have to indulge in the mindless nonsense that our television offers. Take the opportunity to find some of the spiritual gems that hide within the programming guides. There are many shows, movies and concerts that proclaim the joy of the birth of the Savior. The subtle message of a program can spark a conversation that leads to something greater. Use any means possible to foster the spirituality of the people in your life. Flip on a movie and soak in the message that can put you on the road to Bethlehem.

For a Quiet Moment

In what ways has a religious program enkindled a moral conversion within your heart?

Has a realistic film on the birth of Jesus assisted you in meditating on the infancy narratives of the Bible?

_____

_____

_____

_____

_____

_____

_____

_____

_____

_____

7

Come to The Light

Thank God we have been told to follow Christ, not to
go ahead of Him. Even in darkness the path is sure.

Mother Teresa

One of my most cherished Christmas possessions is a picture book
called *The Shiniest Star* by Beth Varden. My parents read this book
to me as a child. In the story, three angels are given the responsibil-
ity of shining their stars so they gleamed brightly in the evening sky.
One angel boasted of how his star guided two children who were
lost in the woods. By following his star, they found their way home.
Another angel bragged about how his star had helped sailors who
were adrift on the stormy sea. His star assisted their safe journey
back to shore. While these angels spent all their time dwelling on
self-praise, the littlest angel worked day and night shining his star.
Eventually, God chose this angel's star to lead the three kings to
the place of the Savior's birth.

This beautiful story shows us how the littlest angel's dedication and humility truly illuminated the light of Christ throughout
the world. The other angels symbolize a humanity that mistakenly
thinks that they have it all figured out. The self-righteous world
says, "Watch! See how my ego lightens the world," when in reality

it remains in the darkness of ignorance. Most of us could easily take the place of one of these angels. We proceed through our lives assuming that we live according to God's desire, but unfortunately we fall short. The gossip, the unreasonable grudges, and resentment are some of the obstacles that throw us off track.

When we read the Christmas story, we hear the Magi speaking of following a heavenly guide: "We saw His star at its rising and have come to do Him homage" (Matthew 2:2). The light that attracted the three kings is far greater than a celestial light; it is the light of Christ that drew them from a great distance. Jesus entered our world to awaken us. St. Paul urged us, "Rise, you that sleep, and arise from the dead" (Ephesians 5:14). Paul knew the horrors of the darkness. Before his conversion, he surrounded himself with evil. He witnessed firsthand how sin had eroded his life. With Jesus Christ as his light, his world changed entirely.

Human beings tend to gravitate to the darkness. In the absence of light, we can do things that we are not particularly proud of. People do not scrutinize our actions in the dark. Jesus confronted Nicodemus with the truth of living in the light:

> This is how the judgment works: the light has come into the world, but people love the darkness rather than the light, because their deeds are evil. Those who do evil things hate the light and will not come to light because they do not want their evil deeds to be shown up. But those who do what is true come to the light in order that light may show what they did was in obedience to God. (John 3:19-21)

When we stand in the light, everything we do is on display. We take on a different persona when we think people are watching us. All of a sudden, we put our best foot forward. We are on our best behavior. Nicodemus came to speak to Jesus under the cover of night, because he was afraid of what the other members of the Sanhedrin might think about him. Many people lurk unnoticed in the shadows. When Judas left the Last Supper, St. John made it clear that the apostle moved into the blackness of the night.

Just as our Jewish friends commemorate the Festival of Lights at Hanukkah, Christians have Christmas as the celebration of the Light. We decorate our tree with lights and illuminate the outside of our homes to remember the Light of the World as He descended into our world. This selfless act of God occurred because of His desire to transform a world that had turned its back on Him. He yearned for our loyalty and devotion. He was willing to save us, no matter what the cost may be. God's love came alive in Bethlehem. He had decided to walk in our shoes and experience our pain. He took the form of the humblest of humans without the glory of an earthly throne. It was in poverty and humility that His light shone even brighter. He lived among us so we could have an example to follow. He urged us to forsake the world of darkness to embrace His light.

Christmas should prompt us to evaluate the way we live day to day. The irony of Christmas lies in the fact that we commemorate the simple act of God's charity with such extravagance. The birth of Christ must become a meditation on how to love others more deeply. By emulating His sacrifice, we become a light to others. We must use the feast of Christmas to bring Jesus to others. So many people unintentionally overlook Him, even though they assume they are truly celebrating His birth.

In his Christmas greeting of 2005, Pope Benedict XVI reminded the world to be mindful of our challenge at this time of year:

> At Christmas, the Almighty becomes a child and asks for our help and protection. His way of showing that He is God challenges our way of being human. By knocking

at our door, he challenges us and our freedom; He calls us to examine how we understand and live our lives. The modern age is often seen as an awakening of reason from its slumbers, humanity's enlightenment after an age of darkness. Yet without the light of Christ, the light of reason is not sufficient to enlighten humanity and the world. For this reason, the words of the Christmas Gospel, "the true Light that enlightens every man was coming into this world" (John 1:9), resound now more than ever as a proclamation of salvation.

(Urbi et Orbi Message, 2005)

Our role as Christians is to show people that a relationship with Christ is essential for salvation. We need to stress the importance of living according to the light of Christ to all people. As those tending their flocks, we should shepherd those around us to the baby in the stable. Like the Magi, we can prove our wisdom by making Him our priority, no matter how far our journey to Him may be. The Light of the World will guide us to infinite happiness. Follow His light and watch the transformation within you. Become a light and lead others to a better life and shine.

For a Quiet Moment

We are a combination of light and darkness, virtue and vice, and a brilliance of hope and dark shadows!

Examine both the light and darkness in your life.

Do I bring the darkness of sin to others?

The true self is operative when no one is watching me. How do you do when no one is watching?

As a teacher, I often compliment parents saying your child makes a positive impression in class. Sometimes a parent is speechless, saying he or she is not like that at home. Are there discrepancies between your home self and your public self?

8

Hark the Herald Angels Sing

He who sings frightens away his ills.

Cervantes

Soon after my grandfather walked through the gates of Ellis Island, he enlisted in the United States Army. Even though he was one of the nation's newest citizens, my grandfather felt a moral obligation to defend his country. Nearly ten million soldiers died during "the war to end all wars." Due to the use of mustard gas by the Germans, my grandfather nearly died in battle.

Even though World War I could be described as one of the most horrific wars in history, the most amazing event occurred during this conflict. In what has become known as the Christmas truce of 1914, Belgian, French, British and German soldiers laid down their weapons and celebrated Christmas together. Many historians claim that the truce spontaneously began with the singing of Christmas carols. The opposing sides joined in and soon some of the braver soldiers made friendly overtures to the enemy. They began their interaction by taking care of the sad task of burying the dead. Then they exchanged food, tobacco and even alcohol. They told stories and showed pictures of loved ones back home. Some men even engaged in a game of soccer. They realized that the opponent was a father, a brother, a son and a friend. He lived as we lived. He longed for his family like everyone else. This miracle made the soldiers realize that behind enemy lines existed another person like them, another human being, another real man. In an article written by David Brown for *The Washington Post*, he quoted historian Modric Eksteins: "It is the last expression of the 19th century world of manners and morals, where the opponent was a gentleman."

Music has the ability to unite the world. I know people who speak little or no English who can sing an Elvis Presley or Frank Sinatra song perfectly in its original language. For the soldiers on Christmas Eve in 1914, the melody that echoed in the nights broke the barriers that existed between them. Music strikes a kinship even in strangers because of the way a certain tune affects us. We can remember where we were when we first heard a particular song. The soldiers probably reminisced about a past Christmas and of the loved ones that they left back home. Music has the power to affect the emotions and behavior of people. Scientists have found that music can reduce stress, induce relaxation and even alleviate depression. As William Congreve stated, "Music has the charms to soothe the savage beast." We can use the Christmas truce of 1914 to prove his point.

Christmas music plays a major role in our holiday celebration. Whether it lingers in the background at work or in the mall or we blast our favorite Yuletide tunes while decorating the tree, music can enhance the mood of wherever we are during Christmas. The music we listen to today has evolved over several hundred years. Some historians trace the true beginning of Christmas carols to St. Francis. The saint supposedly took carols derived from pagan songs and adapted them to fit spiritually into his celebration of the Nativity. Soon with the help of the Dominicans, Francis and his brothers spread this new type of music around all of Europe. As the Nativity plays of St. Francis became more popular, so too did Christmas carols. This type of music was a great instrument in teaching the faith, especially to the illiterate. Thanks to the invention of the printing press, carols reached the masses in the 15th and 16th centuries.

In Germany during the 16th century, Martin Luther's love of carols made them reach new heights. Luther wrote "Von Himmel Hoch" as well as translating other Christmas songs from Latin. Even though the singing of carols was prohibited in church, people roamed from home to home joyfully spreading the message of Christmas in song. The Puritans in England felt that carols distracted worshipers during services. It was not until the marriage of Germany's Prince Albert and England's Queen Victoria in 1840, that Christmas carols would be permitted in England. Albert loved music and especially Christmas carols. Londoners wanted to please the newly married couple, so they serenaded them with Christmas songs. They continued to sing these carols throughout the city and in turn many people learned the songs. Suddenly, the music that had been excluded from worship was now an integral part of liturgy.

The most recorded Christmas carol is "Silent Night." A young Austrian priest named Joseph Mohr wrote the lyrics. On Christmas Eve in 1818, Mohr showed his lyrics to a local teacher-musician, Franz Gruber. Mohr asked Gruber to write an accompaniment to his lyrics. Gruber wrote a beautiful arrangement for his words and that night they performed the song with a choir for the congregation of St. Nicholas Church. Today many people continue to record this Christmas classic.

If you're looking to build a collection of quality Christmas music, here are some albums that will make your celebration more joyful:

Classic crooners:

Noel – Josh Groban
White Christmas – Bing Crosby
James Taylor at Christmas – James Taylor

The Sinatra Christmas Album – Frank Sinatra
The Christmas Music of Johnny Mathis – Johnny Mathis
The Christmas Song – Nat King Cole
A Christmas Portrait – The Carpenters
These are Special Days – Celine Dion

Classical:

O Holy Night – Luciano Pavarotti
Christmas with Kiri – Kiri Te Kanawa
A Christmas Carol – James Galway

Folk:

On Christmas Night – Cherish the Ladies
A Christmas to Remember – Amy Grant

Country:

Let It Be Christmas – Alan Jackson
Let There Be Peace On Earth – Vince Gill
A Fresh Cut Christmas – George Strait

May the music of Christmas lift your heart and bring added joy into your home. Use Christmas carols to reflect on the birth of the baby in Bethlehem. There are many quirky novelty songs that make their way into our CD players and car radios. Some people despise the secular songs of the season. Children delight when hearing the stories of Santa, Rudolph and Frosty. We may still chuckle when the Chipmunks sing their Christmas classic. These songs are harmless as long as they do not become a distraction from the main event. St. Augustine encouraged Christians to raise their voices to God when he said, "He who sings, prays twice." It is impossible to remain unhappy when singing. Join the angels who proclaimed the birth of the newborn king. Rejoice in the gift of His love and sing!

For a Quiet Moment

St. Augustine said that "when we sing we pray twice." Has any Christmas carol helped to raise your mind and heart to God?

When we sing, we lose control and surrender to the melody. Does this music help you to lose yourself (ego) and surrender to Jesus?

_____

_____

_____

_____

_____

_____

_____

_____

_____

_____

_____

_____

_____

_____

_____

_____

_____

9

Old Saint Nick

Santa Claus is anyone who loves another and seeks to make them happy; who gives himself by thought or word or deed in every gift that he bestows; who shares his joys with those who are sad; whose hand is never closed against the needy; whose arm is ever outstretched to aid the weak; whose sympathy is quick and genuine in time of trouble; who recognizes a comrade and brother in every man he meets upon life's common road; who lives his life throughout the entire year in the Christmas spirit.

Edwin Osgood Grover

When we speak about proving the existence of God in class, I ask the students about their belief in Santa Claus as children. Ultimately, there remains one student per class who was told by their parents that Santa's existence was a lie. "My parents felt that if they told me he existed that they were being dishonest," he or she explains. Most of the other students shake their head in disbelief. For those of us who believed and still believe in Santa agree that "Old St. Nick" brings magic to our world. The commercialism of society has exploited Santa Claus for many years. Many fear that belief in Santa Claus competes with our faithfulness to Jesus. They worry that the man in red distracts us from the true meaning of the season.

Recently, one of the most popular Christmas images has been Santa Claus kneeling in prayer at the manger. People recognize the value of including Santa in the religious celebration of Christmas. The omniscience and omnipotence of Mr. Claus is no mere coincidence. Many have used Santa Claus as a bridge to the unexplained and mysterious God for years. Humans have bestowed the qualities of self-giving, love and sacrifice on the "jolly old elf." Whether the correlation with Jesus is conscious or unconscious, Santa Claus fits perfectly into the Christmas Season.

The origins of Santa Claus can be traced to the 4th century saint, Nicholas. Nicholas was born in Patara in Lycia, a province in Asia Minor. Later Nicholas became Bishop of Myra. Nicholas grew in notoriety because of his incredible piety, devotion and miracles attributed to him. As a child, the parents of Nicholas died, leaving him a wealthy orphan. He desired to use his inheritance for the good of others. As bishop, Nicholas endured imprisonment along with other Christians jailed for their faith. Through the intervention of Constantine, they were finally released. The solid teaching and leadership of Bishop Nicholas kept Myra from being affected by the Arian heresy. After his death, the zeal and generosity of St. Nicholas spread from Asia Minor to Europe. Devotion to this popular saint ranks with any other saint. In the Middle Ages, hundreds of churches had been dedicated in his honor. Sailors venerated Nicholas as their patron saint in the Eastern Church and he became the patron saint of children in the West. People in the Netherlands, Germany, and Switzerland started the practice of giving gifts in his honor.

The names for Santa Claus are numerous: Père Noel (France), Weinachtsmann (Germany) and Father Christmas (England) to name just a few. When the Dutch came to America, they brought the tradition of Sinterklaas with them, but their saint had little impact on the New World. They erected their first house of worship in his name. In the early 1800's, the New York Historical Society wanted to recall its Dutch ancestry and they held a dinner in St. Nick's honor. Its members began the practice of exchanging gifts at Christmas. The practice caught the attention of others and soon they joined in the new ritual. Sinterklaas evolved into the more Americanized "Santy Claus" and then into the more familiar Santa Claus. The visual image of Santa kept changing thanks to the literary work of writers like Washington Irving and Clement Clarke Moore. In 1863, Thomas Nast drew the more familiar Santa Claus of today for an illustration of Moore's poem "The Night Before Christmas" when it appeared in a children's book.

Belief in Santa Claus can assist us in teaching the world about the benevolence of God. Instead of being a distraction, as others claim, Santa can be the road that leads us to Jesus. The similarities of Santa Claus to God spur our meditation on the grandeur of His Majesty.

Santa's kindness mirrors the endless nature of God's love

Santa travels the world to spread joy while God's love encompasses all of humanity. Jesus negates the "naughty and nice list" through His supreme sacrifice on the cross. His mercy overcomes the sins of selfishness. God longs for our faithfulness and fidelity. It is through this loving relationship that we gain happiness not just for one day, but for an eternity. God patiently waits our return when we stray from Him. His door remains open; we simply need the desire to go to Him.

Santa, like Jesus, reminds us to think of others

As children, Christmas begins as an ego driven event. What may begin as "the feast of us" soon finds completion and happiness in our care for others. When we connect Santa Claus to Jesus, we learn the importance of extending ourselves to others. We recognize that true happiness occurs with our giving to each other. Take on the heart of Santa and bring peace to others in despair. Santa makes the love of God evident in our apathetic world. Assist others in removing the blinders of selfishness to see the plight of those in need.

God sent His Son into the dark world as the light of hope. Santa Claus brightens our world as well. The mood changes as we anticipate the arrival of Mr. Claus. His presence brings smiles to people of all ages. He brightens our most festive time of year, just as Jesus constantly transforms our lives. Use the image of Santa to elevate your spirit and the message of Christ to fulfill you.

There may be some who insist that Christmas is only for children to enjoy. While being young at heart does not hurt during Christmas time, everyone should be affected by its infinite joy. We should not be fooled by his replacement at the mall. Santa lives. He dwells in the hearts, minds and souls of children ages eight to eighty. We bear his love and generosity in the spirit of the season. Use Santa Claus as the pathway to Jesus in the stable. Make others aware of the connection of Santa Claus to the Lord of Love.

Skeptics will always disparage the existence of Santa Claus. Doubt can spread like a virus. The most trusting of people begin to question themselves. Eight-year-old Virginia O'Hanlon sought the truth of Santa Claus in her letter to the *New York Sun*. The response of Francis Pharcellus Church has become a cornerstone in proving the reality of Santa:

> He exists as certainly as love and generosity and devotion exist and you know that they abound and give to your life its highest beauty and joy... there would be no childlike faith then, no poetry, no romance to make tolerable this existence. We should have no enjoyment,

except in sense and sight. The external lights with which childhood fills the world would be extinguished.

There is no need to peek on Christmas Eve or catch him as he places your presents underneath your tree. The magic of Santa Claus occurs whether or not we personally witness his visitation to our homes. Instead, kneel beside him as he pays homage to the real reason for the season. Unveil the love that changes our world into a better place. Believe!

For a Quiet Moment

We all receive from God the gift of a spiritual imagination. As a young child, Santa captured this imagination; yet this gift continues all through life. Did my early experiences of Santa serve as a catalyst to help my generosity towards others, whereas, my attitudes and actions have changed as an adult?

Santa and sanctity go hand-in-hand. How can you teach children, youth, and even yourself how to grow in holiness by following Santa's example?

_____

_____

_____

_____

_____

_____

_____

_____

_____

_____

10

The Silent Witness

Whoever does not wish to have Mary Immaculate as
his Mother will not have Christ as his Brother....

St. Maximillian Kolbe

As a parent, you would dread the moment that this word enters
your child's vocabulary. It's not the four-letter kind that makes a
jaw drop when others hear it. It is not the type of word that gets
"bleeped" out of a primetime television show. It's a word that symbolizes rebellion, a cry for independence. When you hear your child
utter the word "no," you realize that the battle has begun.

Like many other parents, my wife Allison and I camped out
in the last row of our church with our son Alex. A rambunctious
child at church can become a distraction to others. So we always
made arrangements for a quick escape. We sat on a bench in the
last row that was placed in front of the confessionals. The additional
room in this row allowed Alex to move around more than he would
have been able to in a conventional pew. At first, Alex was happy
exploring his little area. He slowly made his way toward the aisle.
I leaned over and whispered to him, "You have to stay back here."
"No!" he protested. Some heads turned to check out the commo-
tion in the rear of the church. He pushed on my leg defiantly. Then

he looked at me to check my reaction. "Two can play this game," I thought to myself and shook my head. "No," I retorted. Alex turned around and sat down. I was relieved that our first skirmish left us both relatively unscathed.

When someone requests something from another, they hope for a positive response. The word "no" provides an easy out. It gets us off the hook without committing ourselves. A friend may ask, "Can you help me paint?" A refusal will protect our precious time. A denial prevents inconvenience. We may rebuff others because we simply do not want to get involved.

When the angel Gabriel confronted Mary with the mystifying question of becoming the mother of the Savior, her receptive response became the perfect pattern for all people faced with incredible challenges. Mary's consent allowed God to use her as the vessel for salvation. This young woman from a tiny village called Nazareth, responded in a way that indicated her total love and devotion to God and humanity. Our selfish tendency would have prompted many of us to respond differently than Mary. Before we contemplate the ramifications of our decision, we often choose what's best for us.

Our school president, Father Philip Eichner, refers to Mary as a committed pessimist. A committed pessimist understands Murphy's Law. She knew things would not always be perfect. She anticipated that difficulties would arise. Mary certainly did not get a warm, fuzzy feeling from the words of the prophet Simeon when he forewarned her, "A sword will pierce your heart." Mary realized that the journey from Bethlehem would not be paved with gold. She was certainly not an idealist. As Christians, we witness Mary's meditative wisdom and can certainly learn from her example.

Surrender to the will of God

At Mass, we may robotically recite the "Our Father." When we arrive at the phrase "Thy will be done," we should remember that our Creator has plans for each of His children. In a world where we worry primarily about ourselves, we need to focus on the bigger picture. Mary understood the magnificent foresight of God's wisdom. She realized that God knew how her life would play out long before her conception. As God called Mary, He calls each one of us to a unique vocation. Examine your life choices and see where you can experience a spiritual boost. Forget about the economic and material gains for the time being. Mary's example illustrates that, even in moments of suffering, we grow dramatically as human beings. Allowing God to work within your life can scare some people. We fear that we will lose our freedom. Handing yourself over to God takes tremendous faith and trust. Our Blessed Mother in Bethlehem shows the rewards of that trust. Let your Heavenly Father take the wheel and give your life real direction.

Become a person of prayer

From the Annunciation to the Cross to the Resurrection, Mary points us to the importance of prayer. Imagine yourself in the shoes of Mary at those events. Without a prayerful relationship with God, these difficult moments would have disintegrated into utter chaos. Enter into spiritual communion with the Lord at every possible opportunity. You will find consolation in times of grief and experience greater meaning in your triumphs. Adopt Mary's prayerful confidence as she brought her concerns to Jesus at the wedding at Cana. We too, must never hesitate to call upon Him for assistance. In your moments of darkness, despair and uncertainty, discover the answers through God.

Carry others in times of need

Two of our most precious Marian images picture Our Lady holding the Lord at His birth and at the foot of the Cross. When Jesus entered this world, even though He remained divine, His human form was vulnerable and weak. Mary provided nourishment and protection for the King of Creation. As Mary and Joseph roamed the alleys of Bethlehem, they experienced alienation firsthand. Emulate Mother Mary and intercede on behalf of those in need. Show her tenderness to the lonely and unwanted. Stand up for those who cannot defend themselves. Become a shelter and refuge for people plunged into the shadows of hopelessness.

Meditate on the peacefulness and tranquility that Mary brings to Christmas. When we peer into the stable, we tend to take so much for granted. We overlook Mary's humanity. We forget about her fear, anxiety and uncertainty. Sent to a strange town to register for the Roman census, she must deliver her baby in a foreign place. She has no idea of what will occur on the road ahead. Mary always rose as a pillar of strength from the stable to the upper room. Her silent witness gives every Christian inspiration and courage.

Pope Benedict gave us this beautiful reflection on the Mother of Christ:

> With the shepherds let us enter the stable of Bethlehem beneath the loving gaze of Mary, the silent witness of His miraculous birth. May she help us to experience the happiness of Christmas, may she teach us how to treasure in our hearts the mystery of God who for our sake became man; and may she help us to bear witness in our world to His truth, His love and His peace.
>
> (*Urbi et Orbi Message*, 2005)

We should use our devotion to Mary to discover the true meaning of Christmas. Mary encourages us to come to her Son and to help others discover Him. Come and adore the newborn King with her in Bethlehem. Kneel beside her in contemplation and prayer. Use the stable as a source of strength in times of question. Seek Mary's understanding in your moments of doubt. Stop questioning everything in your life and surrender yourself to God. Let Him do great things in your life. Permit Mary's hope to carry you as she cradled our Savior safely in her arms from Bethlehem to Egypt.

For a Quiet Moment

Mary gives birth to Jesus. Do I allow Jesus to be born within my own heart?

"Hail Mary, full of grace, the Lord is with you." Do I realize that Jesus is with me as He is with Mary?

Mary is not only the perfect mother; she's also the true companion and disciple of Jesus. This means that:

Mary trusts in God. Do I?

Mary surrenders herself to God's mission. Do I?

Mary forsakes selfishness. Do I?

Mary says "Yes, for better or worse." Do I?

_____

_____

_____

_____

_____

_____

_____

11

O Christmas Tree

Never worry about the size of your Christmas tree.
In the eyes of children, they are all 30 feet tall.
Larry Wilde

Twenty years ago, my father and I started our family tradition of cutting down a tree for Christmas. We would journey to Trumbull, Connecticut, which is located about an hour and a half from our home on Long Island. My friends heard of our adventures and they asked if they could join us the next year. Before long, more than a dozen of us would venture to the hills of the Jones Tree Farm in pursuit of the perfect tree. They say that beauty lies in the eye of the beholder and my friend Rob loved the "Charlie Brown" variety. We always joked and said that he could carry his tree in his pocket. Personally, I prefer a fat tree that takes up most of the living room. Choosing a large tree had its downside. If you went to the farm on a day that the tractor wasn't transporting trees from the back acres, you would have to drag the tree nearly a mile down the hill to the car. No matter which tree we preferred, my friends and I always found a tree that suited our taste.

We had many great times while picking out the perfect tree. In 1989, as my father and I discussed the merits of a certain tree, a young buck that had awakened to the sound of our voices jumped between us as he made his escape. I then understood how "grandma got run over by a reindeer" and how one could perish from such an incident. Each year, more and more people joined us on our trip to cut down a tree because it was an opportunity to spend time together as we prepared for Christmas. It took the ordinary task of choosing a Christmas tree and made it a community event. Today, our entire family makes the yearly trek to Connecticut. It is a family tradition that we cherish. There is no need to mark the calendar each year because everyone in my family knows that on the Friday after Thanksgiving, we will all be going to Connecticut to cut down our trees.

Historians explain that the Romans celebrated Saturnalia (the feast of the winter solstice) by decorating their homes with greens. The Romans as well as the ancient Egyptians used evergreens as symbols of eternal life. Later, the life of St. Boniface is intertwined with the legend of the first use of the Christmas tree. Boniface supposedly encountered some pagans using an oak tree as part of their worship. Furious at the sight of idolatry, he chopped down the tree. Legend tells us that in its place grew a young fir tree. Others say that Boniface used the triangular shape of the evergreen tree as a symbol of the Holy Trinity and taught that the tree reminded us of God's eternal love.

In 1510, the first documented Christmas tree came from Latvia. Local merchants decorated trees with flowers as a devotion to the Blessed Mother. Around the same time, Martin Luther illuminated a tree with candles to honor the birth of the Christ child. In 1530, records indicate that trees were sold in the German territory of Alsace in the marketplace. They were limited to four feet tall and were left undecorated in their homes. Germans latched onto the tradition of the Christmas tree and later adorned trees with apples. Germans also invented tinsel to enhance the candlelight on the tree.

America received many of its traditions from Europe by way of immigration. People preferred larger trees, so they chose them instead of the tabletop variety if they had the space in their homes. Just as Prince Albert and Queen Victoria made Christmas carols popular in England, when an illustration appeared in a London paper of the royal family in front of a tree, the trend of owning a tree became popular in England as well as the eastern part of the United States. When glass ornaments began to be imported into England and America, the more decorations you placed on your tree, the higher your status became.

Soon after the discovery of electricity, Edward Johnson invented lights (in 1882) especially for the Christmas tree. This fascinated many Americans who were now drawn to purchasing a tree for their home. Christmas trees became so popular that the country's natural resource of evergreens declined. Theodore Roosevelt wanted to stop the practice of cutting down millions of trees for Christmas. In 1901, his sons intervened and enlisted conservationist Gifford Pinchot to persuade the president that with care, this tradition would not harm our forests. That same year, Christmas tree farms were started because of the growing demand.

For many, the Christmas tree takes its place each December in the center of the home. Our Christmas tree becomes not only the focal point of our decorations, but also a symbol of generosity as we place our gifts underneath it. In December of 2004, Pope John Paul II explained:

> The Christmas tree is an ancient custom that exalts the value of life because the evergreen tree remains unchanged through the harshness of winter. When gifts are arranged under the tree, it becomes a symbol of the tree of life, a figure of Christ, God's greatest gift to all men.

The tree has the ability to bring the entire family together. We take our part each year in the ritual of carefully placing family treasures upon the tree. Our ornaments connect generations and preserve memories. Gather around your tree and appreciate the magic of the season. Use your tree to contemplate the infinite nature of God. Gaze upon the lights and think about how you may continue to illuminate the world even in the darkest times. Allow your "tree of life" to lead you, as John Paul II urged us, to "exchange not just material items, but rather, the spiritual goods of brotherhood and love." Let the strength of the evergreen remind you of Christ who remained strong even in His greatest moments of difficulty. Learn to rely on the enduring fortitude of the Lord and trust in His steadfast and unchanging love.

For a Quiet Moment

Faith reminds us that a Christmas tree is more than just a place to leave gifts. Use your spiritual imagination to recall family and faith experiences that surrounded your tree during the Christmas season.

As believers, we cherish the Christmas tree filled with lights knowing that they remind us that Jesus is the Light of the World. At the same time, we live in a country that is afraid of the truth of the Christmas tree and has declared it a secular symbol. What can you do to keep the truth of the Christmas tree alive and be sure that all religious symbols are accepted for what they are?

_____

_____

_____

_____

_____

_____

_____

12

All in the Family

> You don't choose your family. They are God's gift to
> you, as you are to them.   *Desmond Tutu*

As a child, I slept upstairs in our home by myself. On Christmas
morning, I called out to my parents to check whether it was time
to come downstairs to see what Santa had brought us. This yearly
ritual began just before dawn. My parents would usually send me
back to bed until a respectable hour. When the signal was finally
given, I tore downstairs and ripped open my presents with my sister. After we had opened all of our presents, we ate our breakfast
together. Before you knew it, we were packing the car and head-
ing up to the Bronx to my grandparents' apartment on University
Avenue. My mother's entire side of her family would gather every
Christmas. I remember these Christmases well. The presents, the
food, the traveling and the family crammed into one unbelievable
day. These celebrations were precious, and no one in our family
would trade them for all of the money in the world.

As children, we did not know how much pressure the holidays
placed on our parents. Today when I look back on the celebrations,
I know why my parents finally decided to stay home for Christmas.
It becomes too much to handle. Many people have sat in traffic for

hours on a holiday. Too many of us have choked down one meal, so that we may head out to our next destination. We have all looked at the guest list and realized that we have invited too many people for what began as an "intimate" gathering.

The most stressful part of Christmas can be our interaction with family. Relationships can be difficult at times. The stress of the holidays can enhance our relational obstacles. Putting two or more people in a room who struggle to coexist can be disastrous during Christmas. Forced socialization does not have to mean that our relationships will suffer further damage. Advent and Christmas should help us to develop our family bonds.

Pope John Paul II reminded the world of the importance of the family to Jesus in his Christmas message of 1994:

> The Son of God, conceived by the power of the Holy Spirit in the womb of the Immaculate Virgin Mary and born in the stable at Bethlehem, chose to enter the world within a family, the Holy Family of Nazareth. Before the crib, the eyes of the heart and of faith look intently upon this Family: upon Jesus, Mary and Joseph. During the whole Christmas period our eyes will rejoice at the mystery of the Holy Family, just as children rejoice when they look at the crib, recognizing in it a kind of prototype of their own family, the family within which they came into the world. How many cribs there are in the world! In churches, in public squares, as here in St. Peter's Square, in homes and even in workplaces. The Birth of the Lord gladdens us; the mystery of the Holy Family gladdens it.

Practice patience

The chaos of Christmas can cause us to lose our temper, especially with the ones we love the most. Take into consideration that others are under the same stress as you. When people do not seem to be rising to the occasion, there may be a simple reason lying underneath the surface. Spend time to ensure the spiritual well-being of those around you. Think twice about jumping down someone's throat when things don't go well. When you feel your patience slipping away, count to ten before flying off the handle. Put yourself in the shoes of others to understand their perspective.

Be inclusive in your activities

Use Christmas to foster a deeper sense of family and community. The more people involved in your celebrations, the more joyful they can become. When you set out to decorate, cook or plan your party, give everyone a task. People will enjoy the rewards of accomplishing the project together. Alienation can be initiated by an unintentional oversight. Check to make sure that everyone has been included. As the saying goes, "It's always nice to be asked." Assist your family as they complete their Christmas errands. Your presence in the process of shopping, wrapping presents and cooking will ease another's burdens.

Learn the art of compromise

Some people would love to stay in their own home for Christmas while others love to visit. Take turns hosting your family. The person who everyone assumes loves to cook, may enjoy a year off from kitchen duty. Find a compromise in everything from planning menus to choosing how to decorate your home. We must take into consideration the views and opinions of others. The wisest people realize that it is better to bend than to break. Every solid relationship is founded on compromise. Stop the endless bickering by allowing others to be heard. Push away the "all or nothing" mentality and give a little! Compromise will show others our mutual respect for them.

Reconcile your relationships

Advent and Christmas should be seasons of reconciliation. Utilize this time to build bridges in your relationships. During December, we reminisce about simpler days when everyone seemed happy. As we grow older, we dwell more on the characteristics that separate us rather than unite us. Spend less time scrutinizing others and more time focusing on how to make your relationships better. Do not wait for the estranged party to make the first move. Extend yourself in the love of Christ to the other person. Start small. Reconciliation does not demand that your relationship be reinstated to the old status immediately. Stop carrying grudges that prevent you from living joyfully. How can we properly adore the newborn Christ when we shut others out in the cold?

Extend your family to include those who are alone

For many years at my family's Christmas table, people have been included because they have had nowhere else to go. A holiday can accentuate loneliness. Open your home to those who need the comfort of friendly conversation and companionship. You can use Christmas as a moment to teach compassion to the members of your family. Look out for the neighbor who rarely gets any visitors. Offer an invitation to the divorced and grieving. Create a home that welcomes everyone. The lights on your tree will seem brighter and the smiles of your family will be wider. Touch the hearts of your family while touching the hearts of others.

Manage a sane pace as you prepare for Christmas

Stress builds when exhaustion sets in. Keep your holidays sensible by cutting out the excessive and meaningless things leading up to Christmas. We put demands on our family that they may not be able to fulfill. Make your objective spending quality time together and enjoying real communication. God considers the family so sacred that He makes it the centerpiece of His Son's foundation on earth. The Father calls each of us to adopt the child in Bethlehem and incorporate Him into our family, just as we are an extension of the family of Mary and Joseph. Let the true message of Christ's birth resound from your home. Pope John Paul II provided an important insight for us:

> You too, during the days of Christmas visit the crib, stopping to look at the child in the hay. You look at his Mother and you look at St. Joseph, the Redeemer's guardians. As you look at the Holy Family, you think of your own family, the family into which you came into the world.

Christmas prompts us to reflect on our family situation. It makes us long for the love and tenderness of the stable. God wants us to understand that even though circumstances may not be perfect, love overcomes all problems. Make your family a priority at Christmas. Forget about the ideal present. Create memories that will last a lifetime. Laugh, sing, talk, pray and spend valuable time that will bring your family closer together. Enjoy a faithful Christmas with your family.

For a Quiet Moment

Think about this:

We are all part of the family whether it is a Church, a parish or city. Some of us are members of religious communities. No matter where we all are, there is one constant: We all must say to ourselves, "These are the people that God has called me to be with." How can this change my thinking about relationships?

Are there any people in my life that I need to forgive? How do I ease the conflicts in my life?

_____

_____

_____

_____

_____

_____

_____

_____

_____

_____

_____

_____

_____

_____

_____

_____

13

The (Other) Christmas Rush

> If you don't get anything out of Mass, it's because
> you don't bring the right expectations to it.
>
> *Fulton Sheen*

With all of the great anticipation for Christmas, there is one thing I dread, the crowds. When love should encompass every action, Christmas can bring out the worst in people. Customers push their way through the mall as they attempt to complete their shopping lists. People forget common driving etiquette on the road as they visit their relatives. Others may shove through the crowd when they go to view the local Christmas tree in their city or town. But of all the places where people flock during this time of year, I am amazed at the crowds that come to church.

Christians of every denomination feel a need to attend church at Christmas, even if they never go to Mass. We have heard all of the reasons why people do not go to church before: they become busy and choose other things to do; some overlook the importance of a relationship with God; others may struggle with belief. There are even more reasons why people have decided to return to church. For many, Christmas church attendance may be part of a family tradition. But for others, there lies a much deeper reason to return. Some bring their heartache and disappointment with them as they enter God's house. Certain people come to Jesus looking for answers. Some are desperate for consolation and hope. Amidst the joy and cheer of Christmas comes an inner longing for God. The Christian feels the urge to join the shepherds and the wise men as they follow the star and kneel in adoration of the newborn King. We soak in the spiritual atmosphere that our parish church takes on a Christmas. If the holiday spirit has escaped us until this point, it finally arrives as we enter our church on Christmas. Even those who would never think of singing at church, quickly chime in upon hearing their favorite Christmas carol.

As January arrives and the Christmas decorations disappear from our church, so too do the large crowds. In every denomination of Christianity, much less than fifty percent attend church regularly. As life returns to normal, how can we keep the churches filled? Why should we go to Mass each week? These are some things to consider as the Christmas season ends.

Going to Mass affects the way that we live

We refer to Mass as a sacrifice because Jesus made the supreme sacrifice for us on the cross. Each week, we are called to give a small amount of time in return for the gift of His life. Center your life on God and it will change for the better. Making God a priority may help you reach new heights in your relationships. Break the chains of selfishness that keep you from visiting Him weekly. Practice the love of His sacrifice in every aspect of your life.

Receive the gift that keeps on giving

Receive Jesus in the Eucharist as often as you can. The Eucharist will open your life up to Jesus in ways that you never imagined. The sacrament puts us in true communion with God and others. Experience a transformation in your life by making Holy Communion a regular practice. He invited each one of His disciples to become part of this incredible gift. Do not refuse the invitation.

The family that prays together stays together

Bring your family to the family reunion that occurs weekly. Jesus established the Church to unite us with Him and one another. He knew of our need to retreat from our daily activities. Construct a foundation that you can build your family upon. A relationship with God will counter the poisonous message spread by our culture. Make the Gospel part of your family story.

Regular attendance at Mass has a profound effect on marriage as well. Studies have shown that couples that share a faith life are 20 to 25% less likely to divorce than couples that do not go to Mass regularly. Discover true love in your life with a deeper relationship with God.

Find the peace of Christmas year-round

Placing yourself in the presence of Christ helps you to discover inner solace. God wants us to come to Him so He can carry our burdens when the weight becomes too much for us to bear. Bring the cares of your world with you when you come to Mass. Quiet time with God enables us to hear His voice. Transfer the kindness and gentleness of this season into your life.

If you have been away from church, use Christmas as the beginning of a new chapter in your faith life. If you regularly attend Mass, encourage others to come with you as you celebrate the birth of Jesus. Remember that the joy that comes from going to Mass does not end with Christmas. The infinite nature of God's love continues with every celebration at His altar.

I explain to my students that the process of going to church is much like entering the ocean. A person may consider that they are in the ocean as they stand waist deep in the water. But your body can't acclimate to the temperature of the water as the cold waves smack against you. Besides, getting knocked down by the giant swells is never fun. You do not truly enjoy the water until you dive in. The same can be said about attending Mass. We may never be fulfilled by church until we immerse ourselves into the experience. Throw yourself in and see how going to church changes you.

Christmas marks the beginning of God's physical presence in our world. Through His birth, He gives us the example of His humility; in His ministry, He handed on a lesson on living; dying He gave us everything He had. By missing Mass, we bypass the weekly witness and testimony to God's love. Follow Jesus as He grows from baby to man through the liturgical year. Learn to appreciate the means that Jesus Himself gave us to become closer to Him. In the coldest days of winter or the hottest days of summer, make a true effort to visit His house. We must end the bad habit of making excuses for why we have missed yet another week. We must remove the obstacles of selfishness and apathy and make God part of everything we do. Do not wait for the busy season to do your spiritual shopping at your local church. Maintaining a relationship with God will give every day greater meaning.

I can sum up the urgency to attend Mass by sharing this sign posted outside a local Methodist church: "Church is not a cake for special occasions; it is bread to be consumed daily." Come and eat. He waits for each and every one of us!

For a Quiet Moment

Reflect on the following:

Did you ever begin an exercise routine or a weight-loss program and see how quickly it fizzles because you did them on your own? A spiritual life without support also quickly diminishes. When we fail to eat a healthy diet, we can become lethargic and drag ourselves through life. This is also true with faith. Prayer, church attendance, and the reception of Holy Eucharist help us to be energized through the course of each day. Sometimes we hear that Christmas and the birth of Jesus come with a mission that lasts throughout the whole year. We are all called to be peacemakers (not peace lovers) who feed the hungry, clothe the naked and house the homeless. This can only be done within a community and when we are in communion with others. How do you spend your time in church?

_____

_____

_____

_____

_____

_____

_____

_____

_____

_____

_____

_____

_____

_____

_____

_____

_____

_____

14

Haul Out the Holly

Love is like the wild rose-briar;
Friendship like the holly-tree.
The holly is dark when the rose-briar blooms,
But which will bloom most constantly?

Emily Bronte

Each December, we make our annual visit to the attic or to the basement and pull out the boxes that hold our Christmas decorations. We spend hours untangling the lights and garland before we put them in their proper place. We may supplement our artificial decorations with some natural touches from our local garden center or backyard. We hang evergreen roping, holly, stockings and mistletoe around the house. We open the box of candy canes and put them on the tree. (Of course not all of them make it!) In the process of decorating, we seldom stop to think about the symbolism and tradition behind these items. In this chapter, we will devote some time discussing some of the symbols of Christmas.

Holly

Holly has long been seen as a symbol of good fortune. People superstitiously used this plant in their homes to ward off witches and lightning strikes. Because the holly leaves resembled the sharpness of the thorns in the crown of Christ, Christians used it as a symbol of His Passion. The red berries reminded people of the drops of blood caused by His wounds at the crucifixion. One legend explained that the crown of Jesus was made of holly instead of thorns. We are told that the blood of Jesus transformed the berries from white to red not only on that plant, but also, on every holly bush throughout the world. Another tradition stated that the variety of the holly plant brought into the house at Christmas (the sharp leaves were male and the smooth leaves were female) signified whether the man or the woman would rule the household that year.

The Poinsettia

The poinsettia was a native plant known to the Aztec people. The red leaves of the plant represented the bloodshed that was part of the sacrifice made to appease their gods. Later, in the 17th century, the Franciscan Friars evangelized parts of Mexico. Following the tradition of St. Francis, they taught the people the story of Christmas through the use of the Nativity scene. A young girl, so taken with the image of the baby Christ in the crèche, desired to give a present to Him. With no money, she picked weeds and put them beside the manger. The weeds miraculously changed into beautiful red blooms. The plants became known as the "Flower of the Holy Night."

In 1824, America's ambassador to Mexico, Joel Poinsett, attended Mass in a small Mexican church on Christmas Eve. He loved the presentation of the Franciscans as they surrounded the crèche with the beautiful flower. When he asked the priests about the plant's origin, they presented the ambassador with some seeds that he later sent to a friend in South Carolina. After the president terminated Poinsett because of his constant meddling in the affairs of others, he returned to the United States and began cultivating the plant in America. William Prescott, a friend of Poinsett, began referring to these plants as poinsettias. Within forty years, poinsettias were integrated into Christmas throughout America.

Candy Canes

Around the year 1670, a choirmaster in Cologne, Germany sought an alternative way to quiet the children in his choir during church services. Instead of threatening the children with a strap or switch, he decided to give them hard candy sticks to keep them silent. Afraid that others would criticize him for handing out sweets during the Mass, he had the idea of shaping the sticks similar to a shepherd staff. The candy now became a didactic tool. He used the candy to remind children of how the first visitors of Jesus were called from the fields. The tradition quickly caught on and before long people in Germany placed candy canes on their trees as a decoration. The children could not wait until the feast of the Epiphany when they were allowed to take the candy canes off the tree.

In 1847, records indicate that August Imgard used candy canes to decorate the Christmas tree in his home in Ohio. Later in the 1920's, candy maker Bob McCormack created a technique to mix other colors into the white candy. This inspired another Christian confectioner to imitate an old English legend where the red and white colors were mixed to create three layers representing the Holy Trinity. He explained that the red color symbolized the blood of salvation and the white stood for the sinless nature of Jesus. He turned the cane upside down to show people that the letter "J" represented Jesus.

Christmas Cards

Necessity is the mother of invention and the creation of the Christmas card was no exception. In 1843, when Henry Cole looked at the stack of letters that he had received during December, he tried to come up with a unique way to respond to them. Cole enlisted the assistance of John Horsley to create a Christmas greeting that would resemble the drawings that he and his classmates drew in school of their favorite holiday memories. Horsley's illustration featured a family standing around a table with their glasses lifted in a toast. The inscription read: "Merry Christmas and Happy New Year to you!" Cole sent out over a thousand cards to friends and family. The practice of sending cards began to catch on after only a few years. The English Postal Service added extra personnel to handle the large volume during December. By the 1850's, many people in Europe engaged in sending Christmas cards.

Historians credit Louis Prang with popularizing the sending of cards in America. While on a business trip to Vienna, Prang distributed his colorful business cards that his printing business produced. Some people asked if his company produced Christmas cards. Prang returned home and began producing his own version of the cards. When Thomas Nast's illustrations of Santa Claus spread around the country, they were used as part of the Christmas card. Cards with the image of Santa Claus became the most purchased type of card.

Mistletoe

People usually associate mistletoe with a kiss. We can trace the history of this mysterious plant to before the time of Jesus. The ancient Greeks and Celts admired the willfulness of the little plant that seemed to thrive even during the most brutal days of winter. Many thought that this parasitic plant had sacred powers. The Druids would call a truce during times of war when they came upon growing mistletoe. In the Middle Ages, people placed the plant over their child's crib to ward off evil spirits. Many cooked the berries and used them as a remedy for various afflictions. Many people associated the berries with restorative ability. Soon after, the English started to see mistletoe as a symbol of love. They hung mistletoe over the door and as a couple passed underneath, they would stop to kiss.

During the 19th century, Christians started to use mistletoe as part of their faith. They appreciated the ability of mistletoe to grow in the midst of nothing during the heart of winter. Similarly, they understood that Jesus provided hope to a barren world. For centuries, a legend has persisted that a sprig of mistletoe grew from the cross of Christ. This story helped promote the plant as a symbol of love. Love blooms from Christ's sacrifice on the cross. Christians made the correlation between this amazing plant and the Lord's undying love for us.

Love transforms a house into a home. Christmas can be the time of the year to give your home new life. Tend to your surroundings with great love. As you hang the garland and put the final touches on your home, spend a few moments to ponder the deeper meaning and origin of the items that we place around our homes at Christmas. Take these secular symbols that people all over the world have embraced and connect them to Jesus Christ. Relate these stories to friends and family to remind them of the traditions of our faith. Make each activity a lesson in coming to know our Lord more deeply.

For a Quiet Moment

Symbols speak to us and make us aware of reality.

Christmas makes us more aware of the reality of Jesus Christ in our lives. This Christmas, think about these symbols:

Holly – Have you ever had an experience of new birth and that of conversion and realize that all things have a cost or a price to pay?

Poinsettias – Peace comes at a price. When a nativity scene is decorated with poinsettias, there is a natural beauty that touches the hearts, yet the hearts can bleed and sorrow can prevail. How do you deal with both?

Mistletoe – Can I change to make my home or workplace into a true dwelling place of the love of Christ?

Candy canes – Give candy canes to children and celebrate the feast of St. Nicholas on December 6th with an explanation of the symbols.

Christmas cards – Send cards to the elderly, family and to those with whom you need to restore communion and relationship.

_____

_____

_____

_____

_____

_____

_____

_____

_____

_____

_____

_____

_____

_____

_____

_____

15

What Shall I Give Him?

> What we are is God's gift to us.
> What we become is our gift to God.
> *Eleanor Powell*

For those who have seen the animated classic, *The Little Drummer Boy*, you are familiar with the dilemma of Aaron who has no gift for the newborn King. Most of us proceed through Advent and Christmas and never consider presenting Jesus with a gift. We become so caught up in purchasing things for loved ones, that we overlook a birthday gift for our Messiah. If we were to venture to the mall, what would we buy Him? What can we give the One who literally has everything?

We would probably try to outdo the Magi. Gold, frankincense and myrrh seem so impractical. Before I explain the symbolic significance of these gifts to my students, they wonder about the usefulness of these presents to the Holy Family. They assume that this poor family could exchange the expensive gifts for some badly needed cash. Our gesture to Jesus need not be so extravagant. Since His approach to life was so simple, He would want our gift to Him to maintain that same simplicity.

Many songs and cards echo a similar sentiment: Christmas

evokes a wonderful feeling. But unfortunately, they are all mistaken. Christmas is not about feeling; Christmas is about doing. Christmas remains just a sugarcoated holiday if we do not back up the sentimental words with actions. Jesus expects the same. In His ministry, He urged His followers to treat the least of their brothers and sisters as if he or she were Jesus Himself. That being said, our present must be wrapped not only for Jesus, but also, for all humanity.

Bring others to the stable

Our role as disciples calls us to make others aware of Christ by spreading His word. Be a herald of the Christmas message. Exhibit your witness to His presence in our world and show others how He can change your life. Our greatest gift to the baby in Bethlehem would be to rouse a deaf and blind world and bring it to the light. Use Christmas as an opportunity to demonstrate His love and mercy. The warm and cozy sentiment of Christmas often blankets the saving act of Christ, which commenced with His arrival in Bethlehem. Mark this beautiful event with your family and friends and remember that the manifestation of God's love in the stable is just the beginning of something even more incredible.

Become a lover

The scene of Jesus in the stable should remind Christians of God's active love. The stable and cross enlighten us to the true definition of "love." He had the choice to mediate our world from heaven, but He chose instead to dwell among us. The offering that would make Jesus happy is our concerted effort to love one another. We must avoid the temptation to gossip and delight in the misfortune of the people we do not particularly admire. We have an obligation to extend a hand when others seem to be falling. We should share our precious time with the people who need us even though we may be stressed to fulfill other obligations. Reciprocate the greatest gift that God has given us.

Instill His peace in our world

As you listen and sing the hymns "O Holy Night" and "Silent Night" contemplate how you can make the peace of Christ a reality. We can reward our Savior with the same harmony and goodwill that He brought us. Look at your world and explore where you can employ His serenity. Jesus would appreciate nothing more than patching up a broken relationship. Too many people allow years to go by because of an unhealthy ego. Be the first to initiate a conversation with someone that has fallen out of your life. Don't allow silly differences to keep you from truly loving others. Quell the waves of turmoil in your family. Appease the anxiety of those experiencing difficulty. Assuming the role of a peacemaker can transform the world into a place that Christ desires it to be.

Cultivate the hope of Christmas year-round

So many people lose their way and give up. Many are bogged down with despair. You can be the voice of sensibility when reason eludes them. You can lead them to a hopeful future by showing them Christ. When He spoke to His followers, Jesus preached a message of hope. Carry forward the endless promise that lies ahead in Jesus. The Kodak moment of the Nativity makes us forget about Mary and Joseph's expectations for the future. We do not seem to want to let go of tranquility when we understand that more difficult days lie ahead. Present your hope to Jesus this Christmas wrapped securely in the gift of your faith.

Show Jesus the new you for Christmas

Earlier in the book, we spoke about the importance of conversion. The perfect gift to Jesus would be to show Him our willingness to change. We must modify our behavior and leave our bad habits behind. We fall into these habits because we begin to act without thinking. Jesus prompts His disciples to reflect before acting. He wants us to contemplate how our choices affect others. Change one thing at a time. Examine why you fall into the same sin time and time again. Are pain, shame, anxiety or resentment causing you to hurt others?

Imitation is the sincerest form of flattery. Emulating Him would make a wonderful gift. He lived so that we may follow His path. Follow His example and reveal the person lying deep within you. Your transformation will begin when you start to see with His eyes and reach others with His compassionate hands.

Maintain the relationships in your life

Christmas reminds us that there may be people in our lives who are difficult to love at times. When your Uncle Fred tells the same endless story at the dinner table while trying to remove that stubborn piece of prime rib, or you must endure your sister's relentless arm nudging as she tells her rambling stories, you may question whether God has played a bad trick on you. We have the tendency to allow people to float in and out of our lives. Jesus dealt with imperfect people every day. He offered us His advice on many occasions: forgive. When Jesus made the ultimate sacrifice, He forgave those who nailed Him to His cross. If we want to endear ourselves to our King, we must learn to forgive. By reconciling our relationships, we strengthen our bond with Jesus.

When you approach the stable, Jesus would prefer that you do not bring a material gift. Instead of searching the mall, He desires that you look deep within yourself and take stock of the true gifts that you can share with Him and others. Remember, we have the ability to give Him a present that He will remember for an eternity. Generosity and love are the gifts that last well beyond this amazing season. Make this Christmas one that He will never forget.

For a Quiet Moment

What will you give Jesus this Christmas?

Consider sending an anonymous gift in Jesus' name to a particular church or charity. Be specific. Ask your pastor about a needy family in your parish. Find out what they may need. Buy it and sign it "A Friend of Jesus" and have your pastor pass it on to them.

Catholic school families can often struggle with school fees. Ask the principal to identify children in need and make an anonymous contribution and ask the principal to pass on a card from "A Friend of Jesus."

16

Gather Around the Table

If more of us valued food and cheer and song above
hoarded gold, it would be a merrier world.

J.R.R. Tolkien

One year as Thanksgiving approached, my mother asked my father
to extend our dining-room table. Instead of being able to add the
usual two leaves that made the table ten feet long, she wanted to
add another six feet to the table. For Thanksgiving, my parents
usually hosted nearly forty relatives for dinner. They desired to have
a place to sit their guests rather than serve a buffet style dinner.
This redesigned table became an important fixture at many family gatherings, especially Christmas. My parents understand the
importance of coming together as a family to sit and eat a meal
together. Dinnertime has always been sacred in our home.

We associate the clanging of plates and the clinking of glasses
with joyous occasions. They accompany the echoes of laughter as
do the ringing of bells at Christmas time. That festive noise reminds us of the happiest events when we come together to catch
up on each other's lives, reminisce about days gone by and establish
memories that we will share for years to come. Christmas need not
be one of the few times during the year that we congregate around

the table. We should look at how Jesus brought others together. When we read the Scriptures, we see Jesus huddled around a table when He truly wanted to engage others. He recognized the value of a good meal and a fine cup of wine. He used these moments to disarm the hostile and gather the lost. He knew the benefits of the intimacy of the supper table. We too can accomplish great things through eye contact and a full stomach. He understood that a person hungered for more than food when they sat down to eat.

We can be sure that Jesus spent many meals with Mary and Joseph. He probably heard the same questions that are asked when we sit to eat. How many times was He asked the question, "How was your day, my son?" Our culture promotes the fast meal easily consumed on the run. We are missing out on what should be an essential component of everyday family life. Europeans, for the most part, still hold mealtime as sacred. We should recognize that eating together has many long-term benefits.

Strengthening family bonds

Our society demands so much from us. When life hits its frantic peak, our relationships tend to suffer the most. Putting time aside for dinner helps us to realize that family is an important priority. Placing us at a meal literally "sets the table" for communication and a chance for active participation in each other's lives. Parents are given a wonderful opportunity to be fully engaged with their children. Sit down each night and get reacquainted with the most important people in your life.

Everyone at the table should have their turn to be heard. What may seem insignificant to other people may be the most important thing to us. Lend a compassionate ear. Promote the art of active listening at your table. Teach other members of your family to take part in the story being told. As I tell my students, "If you want to be popular, focus on being interested rather than interesting."

Learn the art of conversation

Social skills are a very important part of the human experience. The dinner table is an excellent forum for learning how to interact with one another. It is also an excellent place to increase the vocabulary of the younger people present at the meal. Take the time to show the people in your life how to be articulate and graceful. We can all learn a great deal from the wisest people at dinner.

The table is a great place to learn manners

We see it all the time: a person revisits the buffet line for the second or third time before others have had the opportunity to eat. We can usually spot the person who does not usually have a formal meal with others. In the hit-and-run meal mentality, there is no need for the consideration of others. A person takes what they need and off they go. We can utilize the table to teach each other the importance of focusing on others.

We have all had a meal interrupted by a family argument. A sudden attack of indigestion has flared up because one or more people at our table have sat down with less than the proper disposition for a relaxed meal. Dinner should not be the stage to air grievances or a time for correction. Food and anxiety do not mix well. Keep the conversation light and pleasant.

Between Thanksgiving and New Year's Day, we probably share more formal meals with our family than the rest of the year. Remember the importance of gathering together with your family throughout the year. Although nutrition is important, the act of gathering with your family certainly outweighs your choice of menu.

God's goal at Christmas was to initiate love in our world. This love can begin at our family table. During Advent and Christmas, we join our family for special meals. This practice may get lost in the shuffle of our busy lives during the rest of the year. Use the special occasion of Christmas to reintroduce your family to the secret weapon of the family: the dinner table. Use each meal as the start of getting to know your family more deeply. Make your dinner table an extension of the table of His covenant. Use your table to give thanks as we do at the Eucharist. Laugh together, and share the highs and lows of your day. Take the time to realize that every moment that you can spend together with your family is precious. Cherish even the simplest meal. Call a mandatory meal with your family tonight for no reason at all. Transform your family one meal at a time.

For a Quiet Moment

What are your family's Christmas dinner traditions?
How do you share the love of Christ during this meal?

_____

_____

_____

_____

_____

_____

_____

_____

_____

_____

_____

_____

_____

17

Finding Christmas Joy

Joy is a net of love by which you can catch souls.

Mother Teresa

After each Christmas has passed, I have come to realize that the success of each season depends on how I have been able to spend quality time with loved ones. Amidst the parties, shopping, cooking and all of the other fanfare, the most important thing we can do is enjoy the people who mean the most to us. We can pack the calendar with many activities, but without real communication and interaction, we might as well lock ourselves away like Ebenezer Scrooge.

Knock down the barriers that keep you from uniting with others during this glorious time of year. As you trim the tree, do not hesitate to trim the nonsense from your lives that prevents you from experiencing true joy during the seasons of Advent and Christmas. The older we become, the faster time seems to slip by. Use this time of year to catch up on the relationships that have not received enough attention. Do not allow another moment to pass until you patch up your broken relationships. Remember those who have left us and joined the Father in His Kingdom. Keep them in your heart as you gather with those who are still with you. Cherish your time with them.

As we have spoken about in the earlier chapters of this book, keep your celebrations simple. Contemplate the beauty of Bethlehem as you plan your feast. The stable makes us conscious that true joy comes in the form of humility. Bind every action during this time to Jesus. Remind yourself and others why we have come together to celebrate.

My greatest Christmases have been spent around the table. I've had the pleasure of enjoying many fine meals by many fine cooks. My mother, Eileen, is known as a wonderful cook. She was taught by her mother who although Irish born was mentored in the kitchen by a German woman for whom she worked. My Italian grandmother also taught her. I would like to share some of our family recipes that would fit beautifully into your Christmas celebrations. People have various Christmas traditions. In our home mom would cook rib roast for Christmas Eve and turkey for Christmas day. Often, she would make side dishes to accommodate the person who preferred something else. Her homemade Eggplant Parmesan and Manicotti are two of her most requested dishes. These are all great recipes regardless of when you choose to serve them. I leave you with these family favorites. May you and your family enjoy many joyous Christmases together.

Eggplant Parmesan

>   2 large eggplants
>   6 beaten eggs
>   2 cups of flour

Peel eggplant and slice thin (¼ inch thick)
Dip in flour seasoned with ¼ cup of grated Locatelli Romano and ½ teaspoon of parsley
Dip in beaten eggs and fry in hot oil until golden brown
Put on paper towel to drain
Layer in a casserole dish and cover with mozzarella cheese and homemade tomato sauce. Bake until the sauce bubbles.

Homemade Tomato Sauce

Two 28 oz. cans of crushed tomatoes
6 Hot Italian sausage links
1 teaspoon of corn oil

Place hot sausage in oil until brown
Add two 28 ounce cans of crushed tomatoes and one half can of cold water
Season with ½ teaspoon of granulated garlic, oregano, and ¼ teaspoon of black pepper and
a sprinkle of hot pepper flakes
Simmer for one and a half hours

Homemade Manicotti

Crepe Mixture:

1 cup of flour
4 eggs

In a bowl beat 4 eggs
Add 1 cup of flour and 1 cup of cold water and
½ teaspoon of salt and mix well.
Put oil on a paper towel and rub your frying pan with the oil.
Ladle in a few tablespoons of mixture to make small crepes about 7 inches wide.

Fill crepes with this mixture:

2 pounds of ricotta cheese
¼ teaspoon of parsley
¼ teaspoon of granulated garlic
1 tablespoon of Locatelli Romano

Put mixture in crepe when finished and fold one side over the other.
Using a casserole dish cover the bottom with sauce, lay in filled crepes and cover with sauce and slices of mozzarella cheese.

Turkey

20 lb. turkey

Wash turkey well and make sure that you dry it inside and out. Rub outside with butter, line the inside of the turkey with aluminum foil and just before you roast it, put the stuffing mixture inside the turkey.

Stuffing mixture:

Large loaf of white bread (tear apart into ½ inch cubes and leave out overnight in bowl)

1½ sticks of butter

1 small yellow onion

1 teaspoon salt

1 teaspoon pepper

½ teaspoon of poultry seasoning

Take a large loaf of white bread that has been torn into ½ inch cubes, add one teaspoon of salt, a teaspoon of black pepper and ½ teaspoon of poultry seasoning and mix well.

In a frying pan, melt a stick and a half of butter with one small onion that has been finely chopped

Cook until the onion is soft and transparent.

Add this to the stuffing mixture and mix well; this should be done just prior to stuffing the turkey.

Candied Sweet Potatoes

8 large sweet potatoes

1 stick of butter

1½ cups of brown sugar

Boil the sweet potatoes until they are soft.

Cool potatoes and peel. Cut potatoes in half or quarter depending on your preference. In a pan melt one stick of butter, 1½ cups of brown sugar. Put potatoes in pan and bake until golden brown on the side.

Turnip

    2 large yellow turnips
    ½ yellow onion
Peel and dice into 1 inch cubes
Put in pot with cold water
In the pot, put one tablespoon of salt and a half of a yellow onion that has been chopped, cook until turnip is tender.
Drain turnip and onions in colander. With an electric mixer beat in one stick of butter and beat until smooth.
Add one tablespoon of heavy cream and beat as the final step.

Creamed Onions

    One package of frozen pearl onions
    Boil in water until tender
White cream sauce:
    Melt one stick of butter in a pot
    Add two tablespoons of flour and mix until smooth
    Whisk in 1 cup of milk and simmer until sauce thickens
    Add salt and pepper to taste
    Then add onions and cover onions with cream sauce

Iced Italian Egg Cookies

    2 sticks of butter
    1 cup of sugar
    12 eggs
    1 teaspoon of vanilla
    8 cups of flour
    6 teaspoons of baking powder
Beat two sticks of butter
Then add:
    1 cup of sugar
    12 eggs (add one egg at a time)

1 teaspoon of vanilla
Slowly add about 8 cups of flour
6 teaspoons of baking powder

Put on cookie sheet and then bake until slightly golden brown

Cool the cookies and frost with mixture:
Add two tablespoons of cold water with a box of confectioners sugar

Butter Cookies

Beat two sticks of sweet butter
2 tablespoons of cream cheese
1 tablespoon vanilla
5½ ounces of sugar
2½ cups of flour
¼ teaspoon of salt

Take mixture and wrap in plastic wrap and put in the refrigerator for ½ hour.

Roll out dough on parchment paper until ¼ inch thick and cut with your favorite cookie cutters.

Place on ungreased pan, sprinkle with colored sugar and bake until brown.

ST PAULS

This book was produced by ST PAULS, the publishing house operated by the Society of St. Paul, an international religious congregation of priests and brothers dedicated to serving the Church through the communications media.

For information regarding this and associated ministries of the Pauline Family of Congregations, write to the Vocation Director, Society of St. Paul, 2187 Victory Blvd., Staten Island, New York 10314-6603. Phone us at 718-865-8844.

E-mail:vocation@stpauls.us
www.vocationoffice.org

That the Word of God be everywhere known and loved.